SET APART, NOT ASIDE

FINDING YOUR IDENTITY
THROUGH WHO CHRIST SAYS YOU ARE,
NOT WHAT THE WORLD SAYS YOU'RE NOT

DANIELLE AXELROD

Set Apart, Not Aside

Trilogy Christian Publishers
A Wholly Owned Subsidiary of Trinity Broadcasting Network
2442 Michelle Drive, Tustin, CA 92780

Manufactured in the United States of America
10 9 8 7 6 5 4 3 2 1
Library of Congress Cataloging-in-Publication Data is available.

ISBN: 978-1-68556-272-4
E-ISBN: 978-1-68556-273-1

DEDICATION

To every girl who has stifled her sobs with a pillow, wondering why she's never enough…

&

To every boy who has done the same but won't willingly admit it…

This one's for you.

You are loved, chosen, and accepted just as you are to the One who created you.

This world does not define you. He who called you does.

You are not set aside. You are set apart.

Psalm 139:13–16

ACKNOWLEDGMENTS

Mom and Dad, thank you for always being my number one fans. Thank you for continuously encouraging me and dealing with my dramatic self. You always believed in me and saw the potential I doubted having. Thank you for raising me up in the way I should go. I don't always get it right, but you have laid a foundation that I'll forever be grateful for.

I hope I'm half of the parents you both are someday.

I love you so much.

To Pastor Rick and Kim Leonardi and Pastor Mike and Jill Grazioso, thank you for pouring out so much wisdom every Sunday and Wednesday night from the pulpit in LaGrangeville, New York. You have helped me grow in my faith and mature in my relationship with the Lord more than you know. Thank you for being faithful shepherds.

To everyone who has encouraged me to keep writing, even when I doubt my ability, thank you. You helped me find the courage to pen the words I wish I had when I was younger.

And, of course, to Jesus—my main guy. Thank You for giving me a million second chances when I deserved them least. Thank You for choosing me to pour Your words through.

TABLE OF CONTENTS

Before I formed you in the womb I knew you, before you were born I set you apart.

Jeremiah 1:5 (NIV)

INTRODUCTION

But blessed is the one who trusts in the Lord, whose confidence is in him. They will be like a tree planted by the water that sends out its roots by the stream. It does not fear when heat comes; its leaves are always green. It has no worries in a year of drought and never fails to bear fruit. The heart is deceitful above all things and beyond cure. Who can understand it?

Jeremiah 17:7–9 (NIV)

Before high school, they warn you about plenty of things. The time in between classes is not all that long, so don't mingle. Classes are going to get harder, so don't slack off on studying. Peer pressure will creep up on you, so don't forget to stand your ground and say "no" to anything that seems illegal or dangerous. These warnings become engraved in your little mind, playing on repeat to ensure you don't completely mess up the next four years of your life.

What they forget to warn you about, though, are the people who are going to take your naïve little heart and split it right in two. They forget to prepare you for the hard-hit of heartbreak—the first blow to every bit of optimism you previously held about fairytale endings. I blamed their lack of any sort of foreshadowing for the shattered emotions in my fourteen-year-old soul the day my first boyfriend decided I wasn't enough for him anymore. And then, almost as quickly as I was blindsided by rejection, I turned the blame on myself for not being enough anymore.

I will never forget the pit that formed in my stomach the moment my best friend tried to warn me of what was coming that afternoon. We met at our usual spot after the fourth period, ready to head to the cafeteria to munch on pizza and Twix bars. When she squeezed my hand and told me that she heard boyfriend-I-was-sure-I-was-going-to-marry-after-dating-for-two-months was going to break it off with me after school, my appetite sank through the tiled floor. Suddenly nauseous and light-headed, I caught hold of the staircase railing.

She continued to hold my hand and, in true best-friend fashion, added, "He's a complete jerk anyways. You're better off without him."

But being without him was the *last* thing on my mind. In fact, he was so far back in my mind I could barely see the outline of his shadow. Another person stood in the forefront, blocking the view of any other potential inhabitant of my thoughts. That person was me.

As though I were trying to decide if I would make a decent video game player, I scanned my attributes over and over again, on a loop. I stared at a broken reflection, trying to figure out why he didn't want to choose me anymore. *Was there a new, better player in town? What attributes were the breaking point? Was it my wrinkly hands? My chubby hips? The way I sometimes snorted when I laughed? My braces? My athletic thighs? Did I talk too much? Oh gosh, I definitely needed to learn how to shut up. That had to be it.*

The questions swirled with an unfamiliar weight, stifling my ability to focus on anything else. A foggy haze seemed to thicken the space around me. What was this awful feeling?

A hand squeeze seemed to bring me back to reality, somewhat cutting through the dense fog of uncertainty and inadequacy. "Come on, Danielle. A slice of pizza always fixes everything."

Usually, my best friend would be right. But that day, she was wrong. I knew pizza wouldn't fix anything. In fact, I didn't feel like *anything* would fix this feeling.

The pit quickly turned to a lingering nausea, which prevented me from ingesting anything but a few sips of water during lunch, and the rest of the school day was useless. The questions kept coming, preoccupying my mind. *What was wrong with me? Why wasn't I enough?*

The worst part was I hadn't even been officially broken up with yet.

The real breakup eventually came, as predicted, after school, and I thought I would be ready. I thought I had experienced the worst of the pain already. I thought because I had taken the initial blow, nausea would subside, and my thoughts would gain clarity. But his words, lacking sympathy or care, stabbed the fresh wound again, deepening its hurt. I couldn't eat, I couldn't sleep, I couldn't stop thinking about what I did wrong. All because a boy I dated for two months took me off of the number one spot on his MySpace Top 8 without so much as batting an eye.

Following the initial shock and hurt came anger. A root of rage made itself a comfortable home in my heart and spread its rotted branches up through my mind, gripping every thought it could. Sure, I was angry at this boy, but more than that, this newfound anger convinced me to look for blame in the mirror. So I did. And just as it had intended, I hated what I saw. Staring into my reflection, I began to convince myself that the real reason I was experiencing heartbreak was no one's fault but my own. With every confirmation of this notion, anger seemed to grow stronger, as if its source of nourishment were self-destructive thoughts. Alongside anger grew bitterness. And alongside bitterness, somewhere hidden subtle and deep, was an agonizing sadness. All because I was blindsided by rejection.

It seems dramatic, I know. Even typing these words makes me slightly cringe because I wish I could scoop that fourteen-year-old version of me up and shake some sense into her. But the reality is the roots of insecurity began to grow rapidly during this time of my life, and I'm still dealing with the repercussions to this day.

My thoughts continued to be held hostage to the branches of anger and sadness. The more I allowed these thoughts to linger, the more they became nourishment to these negative emotions. I couldn't access any branch of self-worth, love, mercy, or joy to overtake them. I knew they were there, but I never let them stay long. They were merely visitors. But the others stayed, and they stayed long enough to completely mangle my self-image.

Whoever I was clearly was not enough to be kept around for more than two months. I was not enough for a boy to want to hold my hand and bring me flowers. I was not enough for someone to choose me over any other girl. So, I had to change. I had to become enough for someone—for something. That way, I would never have to feel that excruciating pain of rejection ever again.

But no matter what I did, the rejections continued. And with them, more self-loathing and useless attempts to conform to an image the world deemed acceptable. As I grew older, I began to notice that rejection didn't just come from boys. It didn't take long to realize I'd face it with friends, social media, sports, family, jobs, and even in myself. Underneath it all, the only person who decided that a broken relationship, failed selfie with only a few likes, or a soccer shot that sailed over the net was the definition of failure was me.

At fourteen, I was ready for hard classes and sprints between classes to be on time. I was ready to say "no!" to drugs and to stand against bullying. I was not, however, ready for heartbreak, nor was I ready for the second time it happened, or the third, or the twentieth. My fickle emotions were never ready for disappointment because they were fueled by the wrong roots.

But here's the thing—I don't think we're *ever* ready for life's twists and turns that leave us feeling confused, broken, and beyond repair. Even if we are warned about boys who will break our hearts or friends who will exit our lives, forever leaving us stunned and empty, we cannot prepare for the sting of those blows that leave us crippled and unable to react.

We may never be fully ready for the emotions that derive from these hardships, but we can be ready to respond to that initial pain with God's truth—a response fueled by intentional choice. What we feed the roots of our mind prior to these experiences will sustain and ground its assurance, even when all of the branches may be ripped apart by an unforeseen hurricane. The choice of what we feed these roots before the storm is entirely up to us. And the decision to let these emotions ruin or reset us after the storm is up to us, too.

Fourteen-year-old Danielle had absolutely no roots, only twigs of naivety. As she grew and the hurricanes followed, the only nourishment she found was self-destructive. The more she fed her mind with lies of worthlessness, the more newfound roots of bitterness, anger & sadness began to manifest, tangling her thoughts and emotions with them.

I wasn't ready for rejection. I wasn't ready for the first blow of getting dumped. And I certainly wasn't ready for the commencement of a dark, seemingly endless journey that would lead me to absolute rock bottom, a place I never imagined I would ever be.

But through God's pursuing and patient love, I began to embark on a new journey—one that began to weed out the destructive roots and nourish new, positive ones.

I'm nowhere near perfect, and there are times when my mind falls back into its old ways, but I am in awe of how much God has revealed to my heart in the past couple of years. I am taken aback by His unconditional love and undeserving mercy.

He has shown me how He can make beauty from ashes and has assigned purpose to our life that no man can take away. And now, He wants to show you too.

I don't know your story.

I don't know where you have been hurt, mistreated, or rejected.

But I do know that you have a Creator who specifically, intentionally, and carefully designed every part of you. I know that you have a Heavenly Father who sees you as worthy when this world labels you as useless. And I know that you have a God who wants you to come just as you are, with every broken piece of you, so that He can make you whole.

You are not *set aside*; you are *set apart*.

CHAPTER 1
THE IMPOSSIBLE GLASS SLIPPER

For you are like whitewashed tombs, which out-wardly appear beautiful, but within are full of dead people's bones and all uncleanness.

Matthew 23:27 (ESV)

I cannot accurately pinpoint the exact moment that I became a hopeless romantic, but I'm willing to base my dangerously low life savings that it started with my very first trip to Disney World.

With chunky legs, questionable bangs (thanks, Mom), and enough spunk to keep the whole world on its toes, four-year-old me came face to face with Cinderella's castle for the first time. Its structure, lined with pixie dust and the happiest of dreams, stood tall, surrounding the fairytale image my heart immediately attached itself to. Inside those walls, Prince Charming sought the beautiful princess that would fit the mold of a particular shoe in his hand. And Cinderella, with her petite figure, flawless complexion, and dainty persona, did just that. From the moment my tiny brown eyes fixated on their midnight love story, it was all over. My mind came to the conclusion that happy endings are only possible for perfect princesses who fit the mold—whatever that was.

Constant exposure to moments like those led to an inevitable, subconscious attempt to fit the unrealistic shoe that the world held in its hands. The shoe that would ultimately bring my very own fairytale ending of fulfilling joy. Once I fit that mold, then I would be chosen. Then, I would be a princess, worthy of a prince. Then, I would be enough. And darn it, I wanted my happily ever after!

My naïve little mind fell for the trap that so many other people fall for. This fairytale illusion that plants itself as a primetime show in our mind rattles off pictures of what we need to look, act, and feel like in order to achieve our worth. These illustrations, painted by major television networks, fictional fairytales, and all types of media outlets, depict a picture of success that has doomed our society. We, as the innocent audience, see the perfect princesses, petite in structure and delicate in personality, as they achieve their happily ever after. We see the prince charmings, who look like their muscles were professionally chiseled. We look at the images that exude a fulfilling ending, and we long to fit the picture in an attempt to fill our own souls. We rely on these media outlets to provide a standard that is so misconstrued from authenticity.

Now, it's not necessarily a bad thing to consume their content. I'm not suggesting that you ban TV, movies, or scrolling social media. However, they become destructive when we begin to believe the lies that their façades present and attempt to align our own standards with theirs. Because when we do, we are ultimately setting ourselves up for self-destruction and inevitable, bitter disappointment.

Have you ever ordered something online, only to be disappointed by the condition it arrives in at your house? A sparkly object arrives dull, a seemingly large item shows up in a tiny box, a sweater that fits the virtual model perfectly seems to cling to your skin, exposing every bulging inch you beg to hide. Allow me to unveil the reasoning behind the disappointment: the picture that you saw on your screen was simply a depiction fabricated by filters, Photoshop, and carefully selected lighting to hide its reality. The media is able to glamorize nearly everything when they want to sell it because they are afraid buyers won't go after it if there is any possible flaw revealed. There has to be something that catches the buyers' eyes in order to make it seem irresistible. Much in the same way, the media does this for our own life expectations.

We see celebrities with their airbrushed photos, scripted "reality" TV, and fake smiles that hide any bit of struggle—and we perceive this as success. We look at their wealth and the happiness they exude on social media, and we consider this to be the mold we must fit into. We buy into the notion that if we could finally fit this illustration—this "glass slipper"—then we finally could hold value and the ability to be happy. We finally get our fairytale ending, and all is well in the world.

Here's the honest truth: I used to look at the media the same way you do. And in many ways, I find myself still falling for the traps. I would gaze at the images of perfection lining my Instagram feed with a vague longing to become what I saw. "If only I looked like her" or "If only I lost ten more pounds" or "If only my captions were as funny as hers" would replay over and over again in my mind, like a nauseating carousel. I was missing the reality that each post hid underneath filters, impossible angles, and skewed proportions.

Yet I would sit, pouting, with the expectation that these people walked around in a sepia-toned world and never had moments that needed to be deleted. Their hair always looked perfectly put together, and their abs always looked like God used a golden chisel on them, even after eating a tub of Ben & Jerry's. These photos were all taken candidly, the first try. There was no thought put into posting them. This was their reality. And it was perfection. Everyone loved them. And they were happy. I needed that too.

My perspective didn't change until I started to study television production in college. It was in these classes and during various media internships that I discovered the mask the media puts on to produce the best-rated content. The harsh contrast of the behind-the-scenes look to the finished product opened my eyes to the lies they were feeding the audience. It was all glitz and glamour until the director yelled, "Cut!". Professional make-up artists, carefully chosen camera shots, and meticulously edited scripts were used to project an image far from what the naked eye consumed. Some shots were even taken three to four times before they were considered worthy of being on air. God forbid a hair was out of place on an actress—the whole production paused, and hairspray was flying around their head within thirty seconds.

But still, we watch, wondering how these people on the screen could be so perfect and happy and successful and pretty and skinny and confident.

So, we set our focus on achieving their look. We strive to become a replica of these images so that others will like our pictures, dote on us, and possibly slide into our DMs. (Don't worry, I just cringed, too.) We spend hours searching for new beauty products or looking into unhealthy fixes that are supposed to give us a quick, sculpted body. We spend countless dollars and useless energy on becoming something that is based on an impossible standard because we're under the naïve assumption that it's attainable. It's almost like spending your entire life searching for a unicorn.

Set Apart, Not Aside

Side note, I did just Google if unicorns were real because I panicked for a hot second. They're not, don't worry.

Charm is deceptive, and beauty is fleeting; but a woman who fears the Lord is to be praised.

Proverbs 31:30 (NIV)

Deception. What a foolish game we are playing when we look without much thought.

What a dangerous ground we step onto when we accept surface-level illustrations. Think about it. How many times do *you* post a smiling family photo when, four seconds before the shutter went off, you were screaming at your little brother or arguing with your dad? Maybe you have a grudge against your mom or struggle with envy against your sister. Yet, you tuck this negative reality away, replacing it with a smile, and if you're really feeling artistic, a little fake laugh.

How many selfies do you take before you find one worthy of posting? How many hours follow that choice, reapplying filter after filter, unsure of which will highlight your favorite features and hide the ones you loathe?

How often do you pose next to your "best" friend, post your photo, and then talk behind her back to your other friend five minutes later? How many angles did you try in the mirror before you found the one that best accentuated your biceps? I'm not asking this to make you feel bad; I'm just trying to illustrate the point that we all do it. In one way or another, we've all been there, posting a life for all to see that is far from our reality.

Now, if you hold that much power to deceive, how much more do you think a Photoshop savvy agent can do for a celebrity?

In Proverbs 31, the Word reminds us that our outer selves can hide the turmoil within our souls. Also, I'd just like to say that you can sub out the "wo" in that scripture and let this apply to you too, guys.

Our hair may have a perfect shine, and our calves may indicate that we've never skipped leg day, *bro*, but our hearts could still be filled with anger, hatred, and jealousy. We may have resentment lingering in our bones or disrespect flowing through our veins. You can perfect the outer image as much as you'd like, but our real selves derive from the intentions that live in our hearts.

Hopefully, you've caught my point here. What you see is not always what you get. I wanted to spend time illustrating that to you because I truly believe it's important to understand the reality of this impossible standard. It is crucial to recognize what you're simultaneously striving after and fighting against and why it's useless to continue to do so.

Now that we've uncovered the façade, the question becomes: How do we continue to shift our perspective? How do we remember to recognize these glass slippers for what they are—faux and far-fetched?

Well, the answer, my friends, is not as hard as you think: we must make the conscious choice to do so.

Now, I'm not going to sit here and lie to you by telling you that this choice is a simple fix that will solve all of your feelings of insecurity. I'm not going to suggest that every time you look at an Instagram post, you won't feel pangs of envy. This is a process that takes time to instill into your thinking. Like any function committed to muscle memory, its success is fueled by diligent repetition. It will take practice and devoted concentration, but I can confidently assure you that the freedom that eventually manifests is completely worth it.

Set Apart, Not Aside

I want you to try something.

Look at your own social media. Take an inventory of the pictures you post, the words you paint, and the persona you display for the world to see. How often does the world get to see the hurt that exists beneath the surface? How much of your broken soul are you exuding through your profile? How much content reflects the authentic snapshot of what your life truly looked like at the time you posted it?

If you are hiding the reality of your own life, so are others. I want you to remember that each time you start to compare your life to an image floating around your feed or each time you scroll past a photo of a couple, gazing into each other's eyes with complete adoration, lacking any sort of strife.

We are all using images, profiles, videos, words, and music to hide the parts that don't fit the glass slipper. Remember that. Remember it when you start to play the compare game and remember it when you start to compile these images to form an expectation for yourself.

Just as you cannot compare apples to oranges, you cannot compare your reality to someone else's disguise.

Now, don't get me wrong. I am a *huge* social media gal. I always have been. There are certainly benefits and a fun, creative outlet that these apps hold. So, it's okay to post pictures, and it's okay to get creative with filters and angles and fun text. The danger only creeps in when it becomes the hub from where we derive our value. We can participate in its entertainment, but we cannot allow ourselves to become enslaved to its lies.

So, you take the first step. And you decide to simply start by intentionally recognizing these images as just that: portrayals of some sliver of reality. Great start. Seriously—no sarcasm here. I truly believe that this first step is one that will free your mind more than you can imagine.

The next step is a little more difficult to grasp and much more difficult to actually put into practice.

We must stop ourselves from striving to present our own façade.

One of my most liked photos on my blog's Instagram page was one that I was incredibly hesitant to post. I was having one of those days. You know the kind—where everything seems to set off a waterfall of hot tears, chocolate seems to be the only meal you crave, and you might as well have a balloon that says "Self-Pity" because that's the kind of party you're throwing. My body felt like a weight, dragging itself from the couch to the floor as my blurry eyes scanned seemingly every one of my follower's joyous posts. This one got engaged, that one bought a house, this one looks like she lost ten pounds (how?), that one started the job of her dreams. Good, great, *awesome*. And here I was, lying on the carpet in athletic shorts and a coffee-stained tank, trying to stifle the empty ache in my heart.

Oh, don't you dare roll your eyes and call me dramatic. I know you've been there—in one way or another. You may not get fast-pass tickets to the emotional rollercoaster during your pity party, but nonetheless, you throw them.

So there I was, tucking my knees to my chest in an attempt to stifle the post-sob hiccups and staring at the countless, crumpled tissues filled with snot and anxiety that scattered the floor around me. Surely, I wasn't the only one who felt this way. I couldn't be. There had to be someone else. And if I could just find them, maybe, just maybe, I wouldn't feel so alone.

So, I scrolled.

I searched and searched for someone who understood. I looked for posts that illustrated someone else who was going through the same trial. Yet, each post I found that painted the exact cutting hurt I was experiencing, with its vulnerable captions laced with raw emotion, was accompanied with a contrasting image of pure bliss and perfect lighting.

It's not real, Danielle, it's not real. They were obviously experiencing pain. They don't look like an angel when they cry—it's not real.

Still, somehow, their contradicting photo suddenly formed a disconnect with their words. *Why do I feel the same exact way they do, but I look like a truck ran me over four times after I went camping for a straight week without a shower, while they face their hurt with a smile full of yellow-less teeth and a spotless kitchen in which they definitely just baked a dozen perfect mini banana muffins?*

Then, I took my own inventory. So quick to judge, and yet, my page was an exact replica of that very format. I, too, posted blogs inspired by some of my lowest moments and slapped a cute photo on it to accompany my words, just so I could show off my outfit from last week. I, too, was offering an unrealistic portrayal to my audience.

It's like the mom who's trying to soothe a colicky infant, a two-year-old prone to temper tantrums, a full-time job, and a new puppy, with inevitable bags under her eyes, a continual dull headache, and a messy bun that hasn't been washed in three days staring at a mom blogger, who is in the same situation, but does it all with perfect curls, adorable outfits, and never-ending energy—or so her posts depict. Messy bun, tired mom beats herself up because she doesn't fit the illustration of blog mom. But blog mom is exhausted too; she just doesn't show it on social media. She masks it to gain more likes.

And so do we.

If I couldn't find the reality of these hard moments, I would be brave enough to illustrate my own… just as long as I didn't think too much about it. I decided to snap a photo of my blotchy face, revealing an unmasked vulnerability.

Then, I hid my phone.

Seriously. I had to walk away. I was too nervous to watch the reaction that the world was going to give to my unfiltered face. (We'll touch on this problematic reaction in a later chapter.)

To my surprise, the response was great. I got so many messages and comments thanking me for being open and real. I had a few people let me know that the post reassured them that they were not alone. The emotional connection and response that I received from a post that I spent the least amount of time perfecting were more powerful than those I pondered over for hours.

So, for once, I offered an image of authenticity on the news feed. I offered a genuine, worn-out sandal in lieu of the shiny glass slipper, and it offered connection and empathy. It was freeing to let go of the impossible standard for just one moment and to reveal the open wounds that were piercing my heart.

Again, I'm not saying that it's wrong to use filters or to pose for the "perfect" picture. Believe me, I am the queen of trying new presets and choosing the images that hide my love handles. However, what I am offering is a challenge to offer others a look into what life may actually look like. The bumps, the bruises, the brokenness. The wrinkles, the silly moments, the beauty in the mundane. Perhaps, if we all gave peeks into the messy parts of our lives, we could offer a release from impossible expectations.

Ah, we can all dream.

But you see, this is where it starts. It starts with our minds and the mentality that we create from what our eyes scan each and every day. At four years old, I saw a perfectly petite princess in a castle with a handsome prince doting on her because of a glass slipper. At fourteen, I saw rejection because I wasn't the princess who fit that particular boy's glass slipper. At twenty-one, I experienced a deep darkness that taunted me daily, suggesting I would never fit the world's version of a glass slipper. And now? Now, I realize that the only glass slipper I was made to fit into was the one that God created for me and only me. The rest, I choose to shatter, and I'm praying that you will, too.

When we realize that we are striving for something that isn't real, we can understand why there is always something seemingly "missing." You could lose thirty pounds, marry an incredibly good-looking person with your ideal personality, and have millions of dollars to sit on, and I promise you: there will be something that aches your soul. You finally obtained the seemingly perfect mold for the world's glass slipper, and yet—when it arrives at your doorstep—it doesn't fit right. It doesn't look or feel or shape out to be the way you had thought it would. So, you feel empty. And you begin to look for another glass slipper to strive to fit into. The cycle goes on, and on, and on.

Unfortunately, until we realize that the world's standard of success is nothing but deception that leads to unfulfillment, we will continue to feel unfit, unworthy, and uneasy. Until we grasp that the only thing that can make us feel whole is the love and undeserved mercy of God, we will always strive to fill the void with fleeting and fickle acceptance from humans—an offering to the world to determine your worth and value rather than accepting it from the One who created you. This is the very unstable platform that leads to such destructive insecurity in each and every one of us.

REFLECTION QUESTIONS

1. What standards are you setting for yourself, whether consciously or subconsciously? Write them down.

2. Are these standards from God's Word or from what you have seen from others/the media?

3. Why is it important to remember that most of what you see in the media is not a true depiction of life?

4. What positive impact does authenticity have on social media posts?

5. God wants us to be more concerned with our hearts than our outward appearance. What is one thing that you feel you hide from others? Why? Write a prayer asking God to help you in this area this week.

Set Apart, Not Aside

CHAPTER 2
THE THIEF OF JOY

A heart at peace gives life to the body, but envy rots the bones.

Proverbs 14:30 (NIV)

Imagine a dolphin catching a glimpse of a couple walking their dog on the soft sand of the beach. The dolphin watches, intrigued by the way the couple seems to embrace their fluffy pet and the smiles that crinkle the sides of their eyes as they run alongside the pup, its tail wagging, pleased with its current freedom on the sand. Imagine this dolphin becoming increasingly upset that he does not have a pair of humans doting on him like that. He becomes jealous of the dog's environment, unaware that a permanent home on land would suffocate his air and end his life. While he can't physically feel the embrace of human love, he doesn't realize how many people dote on his very existence from far away. He doesn't see the excitement in a child's eyes when they witness his jumps through restless waves. He doesn't see his purpose because he is so fixated on wishing he could conform to another's.

The dolphin sees a carefree dog but does not see the realistic confinement to a house that sets in when the couple is at work rather than vacationing. The dolphin does not see the long hours of sleeping on a couch rather than the vast freedom of an endless ocean. He is only gazing at a glimpse of perfection, one that is rare and surface level.

While it's a silly comparison, we can do the same thing *Free Willy* is doing here. We look at others and feel void when our situations or purpose does not align with theirs. And yet, we are completely unaware that these expectations are unrealistic and may not benefit us at all. We are staring at unattainable goals, unaware of their true lack of authenticity.

These goals are, in reality, unattainable because they don't fit our unique calling. The Word reminds us that God designed us with such specificity that He knows the very number of hairs on our heads (Luke 12:7). For someone to put that much detail into our creation, there is inevitably a love far greater than we can understand involved in every one of His decisions.

For so long, I tried to shift my quirky, odd, and bold persona into a more quiet, innocent, and dainty image. I'm talking about physically altering my voice to sound more like a sweet young lady rather than the somewhat manly vocals God so lovingly blessed me with. I would post blogs that addressed my readers as "sweet friends" and offered delicate, flowery imagery to help illustrate my faith.

Inevitably, I started to feel like two totally different people. With my friends and family, I was the unapologetic one, full of spunk, comic relief, and an endless supply of rebuttals. On my social media, I presented a quiet, delicate version of myself, undoubtedly how I should be as a Christian girl. After all, that's how all of the other girls were online.

Quickly, it became old. It became exhausting trying to fit in shoes that were never meant to be mine. Does this sound familiar?

I cannot tell you how much it pained me to listen back to videos and podcasts I made where I would force myself to sound softer and more delicate. It was like watching an NFL player trying to enter a beauty pageant. For some reason, it just wasn't naturally in my bones, and that was rather evident.

Much like we waste time trying to fit that unattainable mold, we simultaneously waste our time trying to fit molds that aren't the right fit.

God gave me a loud mouth for a reason. Are there times where He needs me to use wisdom and choose to shut it for a bit? Of course. But I truly believe that my calling requires an ability to use words, both written and spoken. God designed me with a specific personality to help reach the lost. And guess what? He did the exact same for you.

What are you naturally like? If a hidden camera were to capture your personality at home, without societal pressure, what would it see? For me, you'd be watching quite the eventful reality show: a continuous reel full of dad jokes, poor attempts at dancing, rare but joyful moments of reading in small nooks with comfy blankets, and oblivious gnawing at my fingers. Some days, these quirks feel like heavyweights that drag my image through the floor, while other days, they offer to be the traits that set me apart from others, the very attributes that make me, me.

While it's important to self-reflect and to realize that some of our behaviors and actions need to be tweaked in order to become more like Christ, it is also important to understand that we are made unique on purpose. Each and every one of us.

Think about how amazing that actually is.

God was sitting up in heaven and thought you up. Every inch of you. He carefully decided every detail of who you would be and didn't want you to be like anyone else. He wanted you to be special because that's who you are to Him.

Did you ever play the game *The Sims*? When I was younger, my days off from school were filled with hours upon hours of staring at a computer screen, building my dream life. In just a few clicks, I was a skinny, successful mom of four, with a hunk of a handsome husband and a house that met my every desire. Inevitably, there was always a bookshelf, a marble counter, and an inground pool to make me happy. I loved spending so much time putting together these minuscule details of my faux life because they mattered to me. I didn't want to just throw something together or use a copy of some other user's pre-built home. I wanted my own special life to live. So, I took my time to create it.

Sometimes, in my somewhat odd mind, I imagine God creating us with the same excitement, attention to detail, and purpose. I picture Him at a computer screen, selecting every trait that makes us who we are, with a big smile on His face.

He didn't just throw you together last minute or replicate another one of His creations. No, He made you with the sincere purpose of being uniquely you, and so, I wonder if it breaks His heart when He sees us spending so much time trying to be like somebody else.

I'm always astounded whenever someone tells me that they wish they were more like me. Don't worry; it's really not as often as I just made it seem. But when the rare opportunity presents itself, my reaction of complete disbelief is always the same.

The reason I am in shock is that I don't know why in the world they would want my spaghetti-thin hair and chubby fingers. I don't understand why they would trade their own sweet persona for my rambunctious aura. I can't wrap my head around them wanting any part of my life because the image staring back through my mirror is one full of flaws and shortcomings.

I'm going to let you in on a little secret, riveting stuff coming at you right here: everyone's life is far less glamorous than you think it is.

Sorry to disappoint you, but it's the truth. Someone may look at me and see an energetic bundle of positive vibes but won't get the glimpses of lonely aches that haunt my heart in the most unexpected hours. They won't feel the burden of experiencing every emotion at an extreme level or the weight of perfection that hangs over my head, seemingly too high to grasp. They won't see the essentially non-existent relationship with my brothers or the disappointment that still lingers as an everlasting effect of the choices I made on nights I can't remember. They won't feel the pain of rejection that stings my bones or the unforgiveness that stubbornly continues to inquire about a home to lay its head in my heart.

They won't see the messy parts because I hide them so well. Don't we all?

My point here may seem redundant, but it's so crucial to understanding your identity. Everyone has flaws. Everyone has demons that they hide and insecurities that they are anxious about. Spending our time wishing we had someone else's life is a waste because that package will inevitably bring you a slew of disappointments as well.

Let's take a look at the disciples. Each and every one of them was different. To give you a real contrast, though, I'm going to present Peter and John, side by side.

Peter is probably one of my favorite dudes in the Bible. He is unapologetically curious and somewhat of a natural worrier. He was never afraid to speak his mind and often verbally questioned Jesus' behavior. Peter was the guy that spoke the words that everyone else was too afraid to say but was inevitably thinking. What a hero.

I'm thankful that Peter had this kind of bold persona because Jesus was able to offer answers to some hard but relevant questions. I'm thankful for his curiosity because it offered Jesus a platform to provide deeper meaning.

If a teacher explains a topic and no one raises their hand to ask a question, many students can miss the point of the lesson because they are too afraid to ask for clarification. Not Peter. Peter was the front-row student who asked a million questions, unaware of how much his questions were actually helping so many other students, left in wonder.

Then, you have John. To me, John is like the docile, confident dude who just kind of exists. He doesn't make too much noise because he doesn't need to. He is confident in who he is and what he means to Jesus. He even referred to himself as "the disciple whom Jesus loved," and he did this multiple times. What a bold statement! I mean, what confidence!

You don't really hear much about John's personality, but I can imagine him to be docile because you don't hear much dialogue from the guy. You don't see him doubting or fretting when the others did. You just know that he was always close to Jesus and that he was sure that he was loved.

To me, that behavior is so incredibly inspiring. While I find myself falling more in alignment with Peter's persona, I am motivated by the confidence that John exuded in a more silent manner.

Both disciples offer a positive contribution in understanding who Jesus was. In fact, their contrast makes their stories more compelling and intriguing. Imagine if all of the disciples were exactly like Peter? The mere thought gives me anxiety. Or, imagine they were all identical to John? Snoozefest.

The fact is our unique traits help offer a revelation of who God is in different ways. Our personalities were carefully designed to help bring God glory in various ways, to keep us in awe of who He is. How boring would this life be if we were all the same? How mundane would God seem if there were only a few types of people that He worked through? Each one of us offers an attitude, personality trait, and life story that is able to enhance the image of our Creator, proving His greatness. How rad is that?

Proverbs 14:30 was a scripture that God pressed on my heart time and time again. Honestly, I didn't want to look at it anymore because I didn't want to face the truth that the reason for my own discomfort, bitterness, and self-hatred was a derivation of longing for someone else's traits. While my bones may not have physically rotted away, I certainly felt the impact that holding onto envy had on my body.

The moment I started to discover that my "flaws" or the quirks that make me, me, were purposefully designed by the Creator of the entire Universe, I felt a wave of relief wash over my body. Physically, I felt different. I felt full. Full of life, joy, excitement, and purpose.

When we cut out the roots that feed on jealousy and comparison, we are essentially weeding out the very things that are eating away our ability to enjoy who we truly are.

The truth is God is no respecter of persons. He doesn't love anyone more than He loves you, and He doesn't love anybody less than He loves you. His adoration for the murderer serving life in jail is the same as it is for the missionary whose life is devoted to serving others.

I know what you're thinking.

Um, Danielle, are you nuts? How can He love a murderer?

The amazing thing about God is that He's incomprehensible. He can't be contained. His attributes are so vastly amazing that we cannot fathom or understand the depth of who He is, no matter how hard we try. Sure, we experience Him on different levels, but the type of love that He exudes on His creation is far past our ability to understand.

So, yes, God loves every person because God is love (see 1 John 4:7–21).

God hates sin, not people. That's where the misconception exists. God hates murder, not the murderer. I know, I know, I'm throwing heavy stuff at you. I encourage you to study God's love, though; it's wildly captivating and emotional.

Just know this: God loves you. So much. And He's not going to love you more if you pray longer or become a prophet or recite 300 scriptures. He's not going to love you more if you dress a certain way or become a replica of the youth group leader. He loves you right where you are, exactly as you are.

Our trouble begins when we long to change to get God to love us rather than doing it because God loves us. There's a huge difference there.

So, can I challenge you to do something?

Stop.

Stop comparing. Stop opening the door for jealousy. Stop wishing away the very pieces that make you, you.

Start enjoying them. Start asking God to use them for His glory. Start being grateful that He decided to make you completely different out of immense love and adoration.

It's here that you'll begin to find freedom. I promise.

REFLECTION QUESTIONS

1. What are the traits that make you, you? Write down a few.

2. Look at your list. Do you like these traits? Why, or why not?

3. Write out a prayer asking God to reveal why He made you the way you are. Ask Him to help you see the benefit in your unique being.

4. Are you currently jealous of anyone? Who? Why?

5. How can you choose to let that envy go and start focusing on who God made *you* to be?

CHAPTER 3
PICTURE "PERFECT"

So we fix our eyes not on what is seen, but on what is unseen, since what is seen is temporary, but what is unseen is eternal.

2 Corinthians 4:18 (NIV)

During college, I packed on a few pounds. The "Freshman 15," I found out quickly, was real, even while playing on the university's soccer team. Of course, I was self-conscious and became obsessed with the notion that shedding some pounds would bring me pure happiness.

I'd spend my days imagining myself skinny, with an endless list of handsome bachelors lined up at my door and countless Instagram likes, which would undoubtedly help me sleep at night. This weight loss also inevitably brought magically clear skin and luscious locks of blonde hair to frame my porcelain face. Once this all happened, it was over for y'all. I could hardly wait.

And then, four years later, I lost the weight.

Sure, I got compliments and social media attention, but my heart still felt empty. I still spent nights sobbing into a pillow, and I still fell down a hole of self-pity and loathing as rejection continued to pop its head into my life.

I got what I thought I wanted, and yet, I still didn't feel like I was enough. Why?

The truth behind my weight loss was more than just adding a few more reps of sit-ups and cutting back on pasta servings. It was simultaneously, and arguably primarily, a result of increased anxiety and depression that my bubbly spunk so often hid from the world.

More than ever, my mind was a constant swirl of thoughts that produced a nauseating hindrance to concentrate on anything but my feelings of doubt, worry, rejection, loneliness, and nostalgia. Literally, I was constantly sick to my stomach. But boy, did I look good!

With every compliment I received, I wanted to scream. Sure, my love handles disappeared, but my insecurity didn't. My joy seemed to disintegrate along with the extra pounds around my tummy. As my leg muscles diminished, so did my faith muscles. I felt weak, but everyone thought I looked *a-ma-zing*! Couldn't they see the emotional pain I was in? Why didn't I feel any better?

We think we know what will bring us joy. We imagine our lives in a different place and decide that the next "thing" will solve our problems. Then, we get that thing, or we reach that goal, and the once-glamorous look of it coincides with the harsh, empty reality that cannot fill our voids. Then, we decide that this emptiness is a result of our own doing. We are the reason we feel this way. There's still something missing, something wrong with who we are. So, we fixate on the next thing.

But the honest truth is that no thing, person, or place will fill our heart's aches and longings like Christ can. Of course, the enemy wants us to focus on what we're lacking in order to distract us from the realization that we only need Christ. Until we realize that every piece of us can only be satisfied through the filling of His presence, we will waste our time yearning after temporary fixes.

It's like filling your car's gas tank with water. The water offers a feeling of fulfillment, but your car will remain stagnant, and your frustration will emerge as you realize that the water is useless.

What have you been seeking after to fill your tank?

Recently, I got a dog.

Ever since I was little, I have wanted my own fur baby. We had a family dog when I was younger, named Jeter, who I didn't count as an actual dog. He was a greyhound who slept more than he did anything else and did not enjoy human touch. Essentially, he was an oversized cat.

So, I set my heart on getting a dog of my own that would cuddle me, play with me, and offer me a tangible glimpse of unconditional love.

And that is exactly the kind of dog I rescued about three weeks ago.

When I was at the shelter, I immediately fell in love with her. Molly Rue was everything I imagined my own pup to be and more. She was gentle, playful in spirit, and extremely sweet. She didn't bark once, and her fur hardly left any trace of her existence behind. She was already potty-trained, I was told, and she was tame, docile, and precious. I couldn't have written the script better myself. God must have been blessing my socks off.

Well.

Miss Molly Rue is undoubtedly a gift from God, but…I'm convinced that she was hypnotized at the shelter. Immediately, when we got to my apartment, she began running around like a toddler who raided a stash of Pixie Stix and bit at *everything*. She chewed my socks, my sweatshirts, my brand-new couch, my carefully selected throw pillows, and the legs of my kitchen table. She let out a howling cry as I crated her to leave for work and even looked me in the eyes as she peed on my rug. What happened to the sweet, innocent angel I met at the shelter?

All of this behavior, I realize now, is good because it's a sign that she's happy and excited about her new home. However, in those first few weeks, I wanted to pull my hair out. I still have those moments. Essentially, my entire life has completely changed.

I have to make my schedule around Miss Molly's bathroom breaks, and I can't let her out of my sight. Writing in my journal has become a game of attempting to stifle her from eating my pen, and she has mistakenly taken my Bible for her dinner quite a few times. Quiet time with God has turned into a babysitting gig gone rogue.

I don't walk her, she walks me, and her ability to hold her business outside should be noted in the *Guinness Book of World Records*. There's no such thing as a quick potty break with this one. This means allotting an extra hour to my morning routine, just in case. Which also means one less hour of sleep.

I'm exhausted. My life is not simply mine anymore. And what I thought would be the greatest joy has simultaneously brought immense responsibility, selfless sacrifice, and increased physical demands into my life, all at once.

I don't regret rescuing my Molly one bit, but learning to be her mommy does not look the way I thought it would. It's a lot harder than I thought it would be. While she brings me comfort, joy, and lots of laughs, I still don't feel completely whole with her in my life. In fact, I find myself yearning for something else to fill my heart.

We all do this, don't we? We pray and pray and pray for the thing that we believe will bring our happiness, and then when it's ours, and we realize its shine is dimmer than we anticipated, we look to the next thing. And on and on, the cycle goes.

I believe God designed this on purpose. No, I'm not suggesting it's a sick, twisted game He's playing up there; I truly believe that He wants us to experience the emptiness of our fleshly desires in order to contrast the wholeness that His presence, and only His presence, offers us. If these things that we yearn for truly filled our souls, we wouldn't need God. And until we understand that He is the only one who can fill these voids, we will continue to feel empty.

Okay, before you stone me, hear me out. I'm not saying that you shouldn't pay attention to your heart's desires or that you should get rid of your adorable furry friend. I'm not suggesting that seeking a love story is a sin or that you should stop working out because weight loss is not going to make you happy. Most of these things do provide joy when they are obtained in the right way. But until we accept that this joy is temporary and not one that we should rely on to keep ourselves filled, we will always taste the disappointment in them.

God longs to give us the things that we desire deep in our hearts. Psalm 37:4 (NIV) says, "Delight yourself in the Lord, and he will give you the desires of your heart." He knows us better than anyone, even ourselves. But the key part of this verse is in the order that it's presented. First, we must delight in the Lord, then our hearts' desires will be filled. And as we begin to seek Him more and more, the more our desires will align with His.

God is a generous God. Just as most parents want to bless their children with gifts, God wants to knock your socks off with the things you want most, even more. However, He never wants these gifts to take a higher place than Him in your heart, and He may intentionally be keeping some things from you because He knows they may bring you more harm than good.

To me, delighting myself in the Lord looks a lot like investing time with Him. It's belting worship music out of tune in the shower or choosing to wake up fifteen minutes earlier to fill your mind with the Word before work. It's acknowledging His existence and talking to Him throughout the day. It's consulting Him before making a decision and speaking against the attacks of the enemy. It's choosing to believe His promises even when you don't feel like it, or you can't see how it could work out. It's choosing His will over our own and trusting that He knows better than we do.

So, why am I even bringing this up in a book centered around insecurity and finding worth? Because this very idea of finding something to complete us is a distracting cycle that keeps us from understanding that God can use us just as we are. The more time we spend yearning for the next thing to bring happiness, the less we are able to focus on the One who brings fullness of joy, no matter the circumstances.

Discontentment is the root that leads us to believe we need more or we need something else to fulfill us, and we are not enough without it. We cannot be happy, successful, or worthy in its absence. We must obtain whatever it is in order to finally feel this way.

What an exhausting lie.

You know, I may not have had the slimmest frame a few years ago, but my weight loss didn't magically fix the insecurity that rooted itself in my body—it uncovered it, camouflaging its destruction. Obtaining my own apartment and my new dog didn't suddenly force my lonely pangs to vanish but rather encouraged an intense encore of their suffocating presence in the disappointing reality. I'm happy to have these things, but I'm also aware that their presence in my life doesn't automatically fix the brokenness inside of me. And that's okay.

Whatever feelings you are dealing with don't change simply because your circumstances do. This is the disappointing blow in the destructive cyclical chase. However, when a new haircut, a new relationship, or a promotion at work don't seem to fill us like we thought they would, we are faced with a choice. We can blame ourselves and strive to yearn after the next empty promise, or we can decide that our joy, worth, and hope don't come from material things or people. We can still feel whole amidst disappointment because our identity and worth aren't dependent on the things that we fill our lives with.

Sure, they may add to our identity—like, I am a dog mom. That's part of me now. I'm a young, single adult living in a one-bedroom apartment. I'm an athlete, a fake blonde, and I drive a total mom car. I love experimenting with eyeshadow, my shoe collection is enough for three people, and my mom is my best friend. All of these random things about me certainly make up my identity, but they don't define my worth. They don't decide my level of happiness or the purpose my life holds. *They make up pieces of me, but they aren't the center of what keeps the peace in me.*

I hope you're starting to see the pattern here. I hope you're starting to realize that everything you are comparing yourself to, holding your own life standard to, or yearning for to fulfill you is a waste. It's a faux show that will only lead to self-destruction, rooted in the lies of the one who doesn't want you to discover your true worth—the enemy.

It's time to face the hidden hurts head-on. It's time to make a decision to find our worth, joy, and strength in the Lord, not temporary fixes. It's time to cut ties with the deception that you are less than, unworthy, and unlovable. It won't be easy, and I can't promise it won't be messy, but it will be completely worth it. That, I can promise you.

I'm praying right now that God helps peel back the layers of deception on your life and that He shows you the roots that have taken place in your soul. Just as my body was full of rejection, envy, anger, and sorrow, I pray that God will show you the hindrances in your own journey. Then, I pray that He will help remove them and guide you through the recovery process. Healing is not always easy, but eventually, the restoration comes. And what a day that will be. I'm stoked for you. And as I write, I'm stoked for me, too, because I'm on this journey with you. You're not alone.

REFLECTION QUESTIONS

1. What are you currently yearning for that you think will bring happiness?

2. While you can still desire these things, why is it important to diminish their ability to determine your worth?

3. Why should we spend less time seeking the "values" of this world?

4. What value does Christ offer us that material things don't?

5. Write out the things that have taken root in your life that are not from God. Write a prayer below them, asking God to help weed them out.

CHAPTER 4
REJECTION PART ONE
IT'S NOT YOU. IT'S HIM

*It is not you they have rejected, but they have reject-
ed me as their king.*

1 Samuel 8:7 (NIV)

Ah, yes, the inevitable chapter that will bring the painful sting of memories that I've long wished to go away, forever. But what a crucial topic to explore, if only for the evidently destructive effect its very existence has brought on our society as a whole. Rejection is one of the enemy's favorite tools to use, attempting to pry the notion that you have any ounce of worth away from your grasp.

While I want to focus on how to battle rejection when it comes, I simultaneously want to stress the importance of rooting yourself in truth and continuing to work on setting a foundation for your mind. There's a reason that we are diving into this topic after three chapters that have repeatedly enforced the importance of willingly shifting our mind's perspective. What you choose to focus on and the perspective you choose to have are both key to recognizing and overcoming the ploys of the enemy.

Just as any military goes through rigorous and intentional training before stepping on a battlefield, I want you to spend diligent time training your mind for the tactics it needs to face and the attempts the enemy will throw your way to make you feel small. And if there is one promise I can make all of you, it's this: one of his favorite weapons is rejection.

It's imperative that our minds lay the foundation of truth for us because, unfortunately, the enemy is after all of us. In one way or another, he wants to make you feel small, less than, and unworthy. Because when we feel this way, we are vulnerable and less driven to fulfill the call that God has put on each of our lives. How can I stand strong in mercy if I don't believe that I'm a child of God? How can I sit down to type this manuscript if I don't believe I have what it takes to complete it? How can I continue to pursue my purpose if I feel like my best will never be good enough?

In one way or another, all of us will experience the deep sting of rejection. Whether it's a heartbreak (like my 9th-grade sob story), or a job that we don't get, or friends that seemingly fade out of our lives, or perhaps a simple "no" from our parents when we ask for another bowl of ice cream—rejection is unavoidable. I hate to break it to you, but there will, without a doubt, be a point in your life where you will be denied the very thing that you want. And then, most likely, you will immediately blame yourself. What an impressive move by the enemy.

I say impressive because it is. I mean, truly. Think about it. The one way to make someone feel like they aren't enough, causing them to stare in disappointment at the reflection in the mirror, wondering what is missing or what could be better, is by denying them something that they felt worthy of receiving in the first place. The one way to get someone to question their entire life purpose is to offer an outcome they never saw coming: one that doesn't affirm their value.

Are you seeing what I see here? The devil is one sneaky dude. He's also extremely intelligent, which isn't something we should downplay. The dude knows what he's doing. But we don't have to worry! We have the keys to victory through Jesus, but we have to stand and fight in the knowledge of that victory, or we'll fall captive to his lies and schemes.

Now that I've fired you up: let's get down to business.

You're now well aware of the faux standards that are keeping you disappointed and discontent, and you're beginning to focus on your own purpose without comparing it to someone else's. Huge, positive steps right there, my friend. Really. That's amazing. But we can't stop there because test day is coming, and our roots need to be firm and solid when it does.

Let's take a look at my favorite guy—Jesus.

Jesus was perfect in every single way. He took on our fleshly form and made it through without sinning once. Imagine that? I can't go thirty minutes without sinning in one way or another (before you throw your stones and scoff in judgmental disgust, you're just the same… If you don't believe me, write down every thought that comes to your head throughout the day…you'll see my point here), but this guy went thirty-three years without sinning! That's an impressive accomplishment. I mean, really—think about that. That takes incredible self-control. But obviously, Jesus never fell short, and He would never have because Jesus was also fully God, and God is perfect and completely holy.

The explanation for all of that would take another novel, but just know this: Jesus was perfect in every single way—there was absolutely no fault in Him. And yet, He was rejected.

My question for you is the same that God asked me one morning over an oat milk latte: If the very definition of a perfect person was still not "enough" by human standards, what makes you think you ever will be? If the world rejected the very definition of perfection, what makes you think they won't reject you, too?

The religious leaders during that time rejected the truth that He was the Messiah. Imagine that? Jesus comes all kind, healing, and gentle, and yet they refuse to believe He is who He says He is. They dismiss Him and get angered by His very existence. Why would they reject the greatest gift that God sent?

Well, there are a few reasons.

ONE: THEY REJECTED JESUS BECAUSE OF THEIR OWN PRIDE.

With completely legalistic attitudes, they were so fixated on the law and the works of the flesh that they missed the opportunity of the new grace covenant God was establishing with His people. With their noses stuck high in the air, they were threatened by His existence because His teachings counteracted some of the Old Testament's religious laws. The truth of who Jesus was required them to admit that their ways needed to be altered. It suggested that they had lost sight of who God really was.

Do we remember when they came at Jesus for healing on the Sabbath? They were so consumed with a law that they hardened their hearts, unable to love those around them. Jesus came to break this very restriction that an obsession with legalism brings, but they couldn't see it. Jesus wasn't the problem—their limited view was. And yet, just because they couldn't recognize He was the Savior of the world didn't mean that Jesus wasn't exactly that...

Maybe someone has rejected you at work. Maybe, no matter how kind you are to them, they seem cold and stand-offish. Maybe your best friend is suddenly no longer interested in your company. Maybe they aren't supportive of the new dream you're pursuing. It hurts. I know it does because I've been there countless times. But, just as Jesus' identity as Savior was not diminished simply because the Pharisees didn't see His worth, neither is your identity at stake because of these rejections.

Maybe that person at work feels threatened by you. Maybe their rejection is simply evidence of their own insecurity and fear, and their pride is keeping you at arm's length. They don't want to listen to the advice you bring because it would require sacrificing their own opinion. Maybe the same goes for your best friend. Perhaps they aren't ready to see you fulfill your purpose out of fear that your relationship will change or out of pride that they aren't in the same stage as you. Whatever reason for the rejection, the recurring theme is this: rejection can be rooted in pride, and that has nothing to do with your identity and everything to do with their own heart.

In the same way, we too can be similar to the Pharisees. I can find myself judging other Christians for the way they interpret Scripture or rejecting someone's suggestion at work because it doesn't align with what I've always done. Every day I pray that my heart will soften and that my pride won't hinder my calling or anyone else's. Do you see the pattern here? The source of rejection has nothing to do with your true identity.

TWO: JESUS WAS REJECTED BECAUSE ACCEPTING HIM REQUIRED ACCOUNTABILITY.

"If the world hates you, keep in mind that it hated me first."

John 15:18 (NIV)

The last person I thought I'd be having *that* conversation with was Jesus. But you know, He's pretty good at keeping me on my toes. So, the moment that I heard the words with such clarity in my soul, I had to chuckle. It was a humorous way to reveal such a profound concept that would completely shift my perspective on rejection.

"Danielle, it's not you. It's me."

Now, usually, this line is used as a classic excuse for someone to end a relationship or a fling or whatever the kids call it these days. The intention behind the phrase is to make the other person feel better, as if there is absolutely nothing wrong with them. The issue resides with the person who initiates the conversation, whatever it may be. Maybe they realized they don't want a relationship, or they have emotional wounds to deal with, or they are using the line as a euphemism to hide the fact that the issue is, indeed, you.

But when God spoke these words to my soul in a local coffee shop, the phrase offered an entirely new revelation.

Sometimes, people aren't rejecting us—they're rejecting the Jesus *in* us.

Sure, sometimes my bubbly persona is way too much for the world—especially a pre-caffeinated one. But I truly believe that sometimes, people are rejecting the light that Jesus shines through me. Sometimes, the harsh light contrasts with the gloom that they may be living in. Darkness cannot stand light, which is why the enemy flees at the mention of the name of Jesus.

Some of my friends used to make fun of me when I would talk about God. And If I'm being honest, some of them still do. Initially, this hurt my feelings. I began to accept defeat and stopped talking about my faith altogether. I thought they found me annoying because I was overdoing it. I wasn't being normal. I needed to change.

Now, looking back, I can see that they weren't rejecting who I was—they were rejecting everything I stood for. And they all had one thing in common: a bad experience with religion.

You see, most of them grew up in churches that enforced rules and doctrine on them that seemed legalistic and strict. They had a view of a drill sergeant, meanie pants God that contrasted my view of a merciful and loving Heavenly Father God. They didn't want to hear about my faith because they had already labeled religion a waste of time. They assumed my conversations would be a derivative of pride, haughtiness, and judgment—just as they had experienced before.

My heart is broken that so many people view religion as just that. I am brought to tears when I think of how many people dismiss Jesus because they view Him as a tyrant leader who hates anyone who does wrong. I'm sad that they missed the entire concept of grace and have this idea that living a life as a Christian is one full of rules and attempting to achieve perfection.

My goodness, what a lie.

The hard truth of this is that not everyone will accept His love. Not everyone will want to hear your testimony, and not everyone will believe the words you say. People are going to reject you simply because they are rejecting the One that lives within you, and there's nothing you can really do to change that.

However, we can save ourselves a lot of heartache and angst when we learn to let go of trying to gain their acceptance. This isn't to say that we completely give up on people and stop going around sharing love and joy with others, but when they essentially dismiss us, we can leave it in God's hands and walk away with our head held high, ready to share with someone else in our path. We don't have to waste any more time staring in the mirror, wondering what is wrong with who we are.

In John 15:22 (NIV), Jesus warned His disciples about the rejection they would eventually face from people because of His name. He said, "If I had not come and spoken to them, they would not be guilty of sin; but now they have no excuse for their sin."

It's like a little kid who hauls off and slaps another kid because they stole his toy. In the wake of innocence, they are unaware that harming another child is wrong because they were never corrected and told not to do that. As soon as they are told that hitting is wrong, they then become accountable for understanding this rule. That's why you don't see many adults smacking each other in the face and crying when someone takes their favorite coffee mug in the morning. Or maybe you do see this—in that case, you have found just the right person to share Jesus with…

Or maybe you've been to a place with a sign that says "No Food or Drinks," but you sneak in your Dunkin cup and a strawberry-frosted donut with sprinkles because you can't live without it. Until the empty bag and cup hit the bottom of the nearest trash can, you will feel a pang of guilt, even if there is no one around to catch you. You feel this guilt because you are aware of the rules, and you are aware you are breaking them. Your flesh is happy that you don't have to give up its desire to fuel your veins with caffeine and sugar, but your mind won't be at ease because you know you're technically doing something wrong. If the sign hadn't been there, you would've happily enjoyed your refreshments and not batted an eye.

I remember when I took a huge step in my faith and decided to pursue Jesus with all of my heart. As I read more of the Bible and deepened my understanding of Christ, I began to see a shift in my behavior. Suddenly, things that I used to do with no thought started to give me an agonizing feeling of guilt. I knew more about what God's Word said, and so, I knew more about what was pleasing to the Father and what wasn't. I couldn't continue many of my old habits, even if my flesh wanted to. And yet, that was the best thing I could've asked for. My soul has never been happier.

This doesn't mean that we won't mess up or we won't feed our fleshly desires from time to time. But when you choose to follow Jesus, you will become a new creature, and you will yearn to please Him more than anything. Non-believers don't understand this because they haven't experienced it yet. They see rules, which, then, leads them to see a picture of God up in heaven with a gavel and a wig made of jumbo cotton balls, ready to strike them down at their every downfall.

Yet, we know that this isn't true. We know that His love and mercy are far beyond anything we can comprehend. We know that God only asks us to give up anything that will hurt us and that the sacrifices we make are really for our benefit. Accepting Jesus and choosing to follow Him requires giving up our own will to serve Him. And for many people, this sounds like the worst thing in the world.

But they don't know. They don't understand how submitting to Him is the best thing in the world because He knows us better than we know ourselves. They haven't experienced His goodness in a way that would make them drop anything and everything they want in this life just to simply be in His presence. It's the freeing feeling of knowing that we are following a Savior who has every detail of our lives in His hands, with the promise that He'll take care of us. It's taking one step at a time in complete faith that our lives will be fulfilling, joyous, and purposeful, even amidst the unavoidable hardships that come our way.

They can't see it because their spiritual eyes haven't been opened. All they see is the daunting fact that submitting to Christ would also force them to take a look in the mirror and deal with the turmoil that is buried beneath the surface. Because in His love, Christ reveals the things that are destructive to us as He helps us grow and transform more and more into His image. This transformation takes diligent work and intentional practice, but some people may not want that. They may want the easy way out, even if it means dealing with the emptiness that will always exist without Christ.

A few years ago, I liked a boy. I mean, really, really liked a boy. Like, butterflies in my stomach when his name popped up on my phone, and nerves that seemed to stifle my ability to talk normally when he was around kind of crush. Pathetic, I know.

But there he was—a continual reel playing in my mind of our future together. I saw it all: the white dress, the three kids, the golden doodle looking out of the big glass window of our white farmhouse, with wooden shutters and a stretched porch with a wooden swing, where I would read fiction novels, and he would unwind after a long day at work. I could hardly wait.

But his vision was different. His vision didn't include the wedding bells, the kids, or the dog. It didn't consist of a life that looked anything other than a bachelor pad with "Man Cave" painted on the basement door frame in neon lettering and a refrigerator full of leftover pizza and Natty Lights. The only place I held in his vision was another girl on the list to text when he was lonely, just another girl to fill the void and offer worthless company.

After months of accepting my minuscule role and diminishing my own value in hopes of suddenly changing his mind, it was over. He was gone. His name was vacant from my phone; my texts were left on read. The snapchats were left on open—the final sign of defeat.

I shouldn't have been surprised because all of the red flags were there. But in my delusional state fueled by lust, a longing to be chosen and loved, and the exciting notion that I could be the girl he "changed" for, I was blinded. And so, I sat awake most nights, staring at a phone with an inbox as empty as I felt inside, wondering why I wasn't enough for him. Why did he reject me? What could I have done to make him accept me and ride off into the sunset to our farmhouse fairytale?

The truth is, looking back, I can see exactly why he rejected me. And it had nothing to do with my worth, but everything to do with the simple fact that choosing me would come with the selfless act of giving up his freedom. Choosing me, in his eyes, meant that Saturdays would no longer be for just the boys and that his actions would become accountable to the person he now shared his heart with. His rejection stemmed from what would have to change in his own life, not from who I was or wasn't.

If I had seen it back then, I wouldn't have wasted so many nights suffocated by self-destructive thoughts, wondering if I would ever be enough for someone. I wouldn't have settled for being his backup, waiting around aimlessly for a day to come where he suddenly discovered my worth. My worth was never his to determine, and his rejection of my company was one birthed out of a selfish fear to succumb to accountability.

I know that sounds harsh on the guy, so let's self-reflect a little, too. There were plenty of times where I said no to hanging out with a friend because I wanted a night to myself. There have been times when I wasn't ready to jump into a relationship, and so, I was the one who cut things off. There have been moments where my own rejecting behavior has undoubtedly caused harm to someone in ways that I never intended it to.

Think of the times you have done that, too. I'm sure you never intended to hurt that person or diminish their value. In the same way, when we feel rejection, the decision from the person who is dismissive of you is more focused on themselves, not you. This is so important to remember. Do we see the pattern here?

THREE: THEY REJECTED JESUS BECAUSE IT WAS ESSENTIAL TO FULFILL THE PURPOSE HE CAME FOR.

If everyone just accepted Christ with glee, there would be no story of the cross. If every person saw Jesus for all that He was, He wouldn't have been sentenced to die. If He was never crucified, there would be no easy way to access our Heavenly Father through intercession. And without the story of the cross, there would be no hope for you or me to enter heaven. There would be no freedom in the forgiveness of our sins. Unfortunately, rejection was the very thing that drove Jesus to His purpose, but I am sitting here in absolute gratitude that it did.

There's a reason behind every rejection that takes place in our lives. Does it make the sting of it any less painful? Of course not.

Jesus endured great pain during His time here on earth, and I'm certain He wanted to scream when people questioned His identity publicly over and over again. It hurts immensely when people don't appreciate all that we are because it makes us feel like there's something wrong with us. But when we shift our perspective and choose to believe that God has an ordained reason behind every rejection we face, it will help us preserve our identity and worth.

Maybe the rejection of that one job led you to apply for the other one that became the biggest blessing in your life. Maybe that one failed relationship led you to a better one that has enhanced your view on love. Perhaps the very reason you lost that group of friends was to make room for another group who would point you to Jesus and allow you to be more yourself than you ever have been.

God only removes people and things from our lives in order to fulfill His purpose through us by taking away the hindrances that will steer us off course. Just like any parent, He knows what's best for you and what's harmful to your path. I'm not a human parent, but I am a dog parent, so I have some insight here.

My fur child, Molly Rue, has absolutely no street sense. She could care less if eighteen cars were coming full speed at her: if she sees a squirrel on the other side of the road, she's crossing it, no questions asked. I don't walk her; she walks me. So, we're working on it.

I've been tightening her leash and teaching her to walk right beside me, even though she wants to roam free all over the neighborhood. When I have to halt her desire, she looks at me with those literal puppy-dog brown eyes that seem to be saying, "But Mom! You're ruining all of the fun!"

Sure, Miss Molly, you may think I'm the worst parent in the world, but you don't realize that I'm holding you back from pursuing that squirrel because doing so would make you roadkill. Letting you free to do whatever you please will undoubtedly end with me digging a hole for your lifeless body. So, you choose. Live a long life with the coolest mom ever, who lets you sleep in her Tempur-Pedic, queen size bed and feeds you dozens of treats and gives you fun toys that tire you out within minutes, or you get what you want in that moment and watch a car end your life right there and then?

Just like Molly, we too can become fixated out of naivety and innocence by the things we want. In our desire to pursue them, we ignore the possibilities of the detrimental effects they can have on us. We, too, can look at God with watery eyes and a feeling of unfairness as we wonder why He's keeping us away from what we want. We think we're at fault or that we don't deserve it. We think it's a punishment—a result of our own shortcomings. But what a faulty lie that is. His "no" is a protection out of love, not a depiction of who you are or aren't.

Whatever the reason behind it is, the "death" that results from rejection is always for a greater purpose. We feel like not getting our way was a death in and of itself, but we are unaware of the life that God has preserved through it. Jesus' death on the cross wasn't a death of sorrow, it was one of hope and unbelievable love—the greatest gift we could ever receive. His death brought our offer of eternal life with Him. What an amazing, beautiful thing that looked so grim on the outside.

Wherever rejection has stung your bones, please know this: you are still living in God's purpose as long as you are seeking Him. You are still a child of God. You are still loved, cherished, and beautiful in His sight. He makes beauty from ashes, and your pain will turn to joy. Your calling isn't in jeopardy. You are still on the path that God has for you. Know who you are, and keep going.

REFLECTION QUESTIONS

1. What rejection(s) are you holding onto? Can you shift your perspective to see how God brought something better along?

2. Maybe the "why" of it hasn't been revealed to you yet. Write a prayer asking God to help you move on anyway. Ask Him to open your eyes to what He's doing in your life and to give you peace knowing there was a good reason behind the rejection, even if He never reveals the reason for it.

3. When you think about Jesus being rejected, how does this comfort you?

4. How can you stand firm in your identity when others reject it?

5. Find a scripture that reminds you of who Jesus says you are. There are so many! Paul gives some great examples in the New Testament, but go where God brings you. Write it down and say it out loud every day this week. Hang it up. Tuck it in your purse. Keep it in your sight and heart all week, and see how much the Word can help us preserve our worth through Christ's view of us.

CHAPTER 5
REJECTION PART TWO
OKAY, IT MAY ALSO BE YOU

For you formed my inward parts; you knitted me together in my mother's womb.

Psalm 139:13 (ESV)

I will never forget the day when one of my friends from church came up to me and declared that I was "hard to set someone up with." When my face returned a puzzled look, he elaborated.

"It's just that you're kind of a strong personality, you know?"

Initially, I laughed and agreed with him because of the validity of that statement.

I mean, it's rather obvious that I have a bold presence. Anyone who's around me for more than five minutes can attest to that. I can't tell you how many times I've made a predetermined decision to keep quiet in certain situations or offered to present a more conservative version of myself and immediately failed to do so. My mouth and body did not like the mental straitjacket I was trying to confine them with because they were completely out of their element. So, in an attempt to return to normalcy, they would break free, reverting right back to their outgoing ways.

For some people, this is acceptable. They enjoy my ability to converse with anyone and anything and the way I can seemingly lighten any situation with my natural awkwardness. But for others, it's too much. It's a commercial with a volume much higher than the program, an initial shock of an ice-cold pool on a summer day. My outer shell is an uncomfortable interruption to the very peace their body thrives in.

And for many guys, this is the threat of being with a girl who may not succumb to everything they want. They look at my bold persona and assume it also comes with an inability to submit or an overpowering disposition that defies authority. While I know that this is far from the truth, they don't, unless they take the time to truly get to know me.

I can be loud, quirky, and bold. I cry over breathtaking sunsets, Nicholas Sparks' films, and killing spiders—even though I'm convinced they are creatures working for Satan himself. I'm not afraid to be the oddball out, yet I simultaneously don't handle criticism well. I like to document experiences that warm my heart most with daily Instagram stories of nature or cozy couch corners or sky-high bookshelves. I laugh a lot. I laugh when I'm happy or when I'm nervous. I laugh with friends, at work, and at all the wrong times. I am not cut out for fashion pageants or debutant tea parties. I will always prefer watching *Monday Night Football* over *The Bachelor*. And I overthink pretty much every single thing.

There are so many parts of me that are easy to reject, but that's okay. Because the One who knit me together knew exactly what He was doing when He chose to give me a tender heart, spunky energy, and a headstrong attitude. His decision to knit every specific interest I have in my soul was purposeful, and He has done the same with you.

Sure, some people may reject these pieces of me, but just because my image doesn't fit their ideal mold doesn't mean I am a failure or that there's something wrong with me. This doesn't mean that I should just accept parts of me that can be detrimental to my life or seem to cause strife around me, but I can accept that God can use them to glorify His nature. They are the broken pieces of me that He uses to show His mighty power in being able to use the overlooked and the seemingly useless.

The truth is, God made you for a specific reason. He took the precious time to decide every attribute that would make you, you. And He did so for a specific reason. I know I may sound like a broken record, but it's important to be reminded of it. Because as much as we say we know this, the test of rejection will usually always bring us to our knees or in front of a mirror, wondering what parts of us are unacceptable.

Just because some people don't accept you doesn't mean you aren't accepted.

Just because some people don't notice your worth doesn't mean you are worthless.

Just because some people don't like ranch dressing doesn't mean it's not the greatest dressing on the face of the planet because it has the ability to make anything paired with it taste like a piece of heaven. Imagine if they stopped manufacturing ranch simply because a handful of people rejected its taste. Imagine the magnificence my taste buds would be missing out on because of some other person's opinion…

I just imagined a world without ranch, and I'm tearing up a little.

The reality is that you are not going to be everyone's cup of tea. Your personality is not made to satisfy the needs of every single person around you because we are all so uniquely different, both in the way that we are made and in the needs that we are able to fill for those God has placed in our lives.

I tried so hard to throw away my seemingly "undesired" traits and replace them with ones that society deemed to be preferable.

I became the girl that everyone wanted me to be, in whatever situation I was in. But ultimately, when I masked my naturally deep voice with a soft, dainty whisper, or I tried to be this tough chick who could handle any insult thrown her way, or I attempted to convince others that I was this go-getter businesswoman with hopes and dreams of having a million-dollar business, my soul ached with emptiness. My life became a movie with a cast of 1,000 different main characters, and I played them all—what an exhausting job.

I rather live one life, authentic and unapologetic to who God has made me to truly be, than live in a thousand different shoes, fostering a life that is uncomfortable and unfulfilled.

God has and will always place people in your life who need you to be exactly who you were created to be. Sometimes, we focus so much on the ones that reject us that we dismiss the impact we have on the ones who have accepted us. Whatever you bring to the table, someone, somewhere, will need. And I bet it will be a whole lot of someones.

During my junior year of high school, I began reaching out to various coaches that I wished to play for. With nothing but my lifelong dream to play collegiate soccer to lose, I submitted email after email, along with a sad attempt at a highlight reel consisting of footage from my mom's handheld video camera.

Some coaches wrote back with interest, others never responded, and some came back as rejections with encouraging explanations. They looked a lot like this:

> *Ms. Axelrod,*
> *We want to thank you on behalf of (insert university name here) for expressing interest in being part of our women's soccer program. Your reel shows*

that you hold promising potential on the soccer field, although we are not looking for midfielders right now. If you would like to consider another position, please reach out, and we can discuss enrolling you in one of our recruitment camps or coming to see you play as a (desired position) in an upcoming show-case.

Looking forward to hearing from you!

Sincerely,
Coach (insert important name here)

I never responded to these emails. Alright, relax—it was not because I was rude or bitter, but because I knew I wouldn't be offering my full potential.

Although I wore the number nine on the back of my jersey, I was no Mia Hamm on that field. I was well aware of that, but I wasn't the worst player to step on the field either. My vision, creative passing, and ability to run and run and run (I knew that energy would come in handy) without needing a break made me a solid attribute to the midfield. Although I could shift into other positions on a need-to basis, I was never as comfortable or confident as I was when I took my usual spot in the middle of the field.

On defense, I dove in too quickly. It really wasn't a hard task to beat me one on one.

At forward, I hesitated to go to goal myself. I was used to passing, and my speed with the ball at my feet was questionably slow. This is why I opted to give it to someone else as quickly as possible most of the time. Oh, and my composure was horrible. Give me the ball from eighteen-plus feet away, and I could send it past the goalie, smacking the back of the net with a determined force, but place me two feet from the goal with a wide-open net, and I will miss—every time.

I won't even waste a paragraph explaining how horrible I would be as a goalkeeper.

I was at my best when I was in my designated role—the one that came most naturally to me—as a midfielder.

So, I waited for the team that needed me to fill the role I felt most equipped for.

In the same way, there will be people who flat-out reject who we are, but there will also be people who will try to change who we are in order to fit their needs.

Don't settle for that. Trying to be anything other than the person that God has created you to be will be unsettling. It depletes your confidence. It masks your full potential.

So, yes, maybe that job was looking for someone with different skills. Maybe that person was looking for someone with a different personality. Maybe that director was looking for a different performer for the role. But God knew those rejections were in your best interest.

There will be a job that will utilize your skillset. There will be a person who will enjoy your company and will appreciate all of who you are. There will be another chance, another opportunity, another relationship. And they will need you to be *exactly* who you are.

Now, I'm not saying that there aren't parts of us that don't need tweaking. Believe me; I have a whole list that needs some work. There are parts of who we are that aren't fully developed or are expressed out of context. And there are parts of us that will have to change as we learn how to love others. But this doesn't mean that we aren't worthy or that we are broken or less than able to fulfill all that God has created us to be.

We live life, and we learn, and we grow. Our failures are the best foundations for learning to take place. But we don't give up altogether. We don't throw in the towel and decide that we are useless. We accept that we're human, but we also accept that we are unique humans.

We change to conform our image to look more like Christ, but we don't let rejection from others change us to conform our image to look more acceptable to people. Imagine if Jesus did that? Imagine if He threw His hands up and was like, "Yeah, you're right. Let's just stick with legalism," and gained the approval of the religious leaders? Had He done that, He would've completely missed the will of God for His life. And if He never went to the cross, we would still be living under the law covenant today. Imagine that, having to constantly slaughter animals? No, thanks.

Whatever your purpose is (and you have one! I promise!), know that God made you exactly the way you are in order to fulfill that purpose. He will strengthen those attributes and help you grow in them, but not everyone will love them. Not everyone will understand you or want what you bring to the table, but some will. And those "some" matter. They matter a whole lot, and God ordained you to be a part of their journey.

I can confidently sit here and type this without hesitation based on every single rejection I've ever experienced (and there have been quite a few, my friends…): God never allows any door to shut unless it is for your greater good. When a child, in their innocence, is met with a "no" from their parents, they don't understand that they are just trying to save them from a dangerous outcome. They are forbidding them from doing something out of concern, love, and safety. Much in the same, God's "nos" are not out of punishment but, rather, out of pure love.

However, there are other rejections that God allows that come from the enemy. And it's important that we are aware of these as well.

When I was a freshman in college, I took a required English class. Writing had always been one of my stronger skills in school, so I usually looked forward to any sort of English class. For years, I was used to seeing high grades on my papers and notes in red ink from my teachers that encouraged me to continue working on my craft. They saw potential, and it was evident that I had a talent.

Well, Miss Chair of the English Department, who taught my 8:30 a.m. English 202 course did not agree. With every returned paper, my heart would sink with disappointment. There would be marks all over the margins and grades that reflected that of someone who certainly would never be qualified to write a book. All those years of encouragement, and I became defeated by one professor's opinion. One rejection of my craft, and I decided that I wasn't called anymore. I let remarks that were meant to help develop my writing seep deeper as destructive words that questioned my gift.

My writing style is not best suited for an English 202 class. Looking back, I get that. Most of the notes that my professor etched on my pages were valid. But, the truth is, there are so many types of books out there with writers who have different voices, styles, and structures. There are people who are interested in reading encyclopedias, those interested in autobiographies, and others interested in fairytales. There are writers of all different genres, and they are all good at what they do. Their styles are just different, and that doesn't dismiss the fact that their ability to write was naturally woven into their soul.

You, my friend, have a gift that God has given you. Actually, I bet He's given you plenty. And the last thing the enemy wants is for you to use them. So, of course, he will try to get you to doubt your worth. Of course, he will make you question your identity. Even Jesus went through this period. Before He stepped into His calling, the devil tempted Him in the wilderness with questions that were meant to take Jesus' eyes off His calling.

Doesn't he do the same to us?

So, how do we respond? How do we recognize that these rejections or questions may just be testing the faith we have in who we were created to be through Christ?

Well, let's go back to youth group days when our wrists gained tan lines over the summer from the yarn bracelets that sported the letters WWJD: What would Jesus do?

Jesus combatted the temptations from Satan with the Word of God. Although the enemy took a shot at His flesh and tried to persuade His mind with his sneaky tactics, Jesus spoke the written Word of God aloud in order to combat lies with the truth.

When rejection comes our way, and other people are used to try and question our identity: we need to stand on the Word. We need to stand on God's truth. And in order to do so, we need to know what God says about us in His Word.

The more we root ourselves in God's truth, the less we will be swayed by rejection, failures, or temptations. So, if you're ready to be a strong oak, able to stand in the most furious of storms, rather than a weak dandelion, mowed over with ease by the slightest of breezes, then flip the page, and begin a journey of developing strong roots, with blossoming branches.

REFLECTION QUESTIONS

1. What unique traits do you have? Do you accept them or seem to be bothered by them?

2. Why do you think God made you the way that you are? Have you seen positive experiences in which your specific personality was of benefit?

3. Why is it important to remember what God's Word says about you?

4. How can you learn more about who you are in Christ?

CHAPTER 6
THE CHOSEN ONES

In Him we were also chosen, having been predes-
tined according to the plan of Him who works out
everything in conformity with the purpose of His
will.

Ephesians 1:11 (NIV)

We all long to be chosen. Some want someone to choose to date them. Some want their boss to choose to give them the promotion. Some want their lotto numbers to be chosen as the winning jackpot. Some just hope they are chosen before they are the last person in line for a team in gym class.

We want to be chosen because when we are pointed out, set apart from the others, we are suddenly noticed for our value. The very hand that points to us, recognizing our existence, offers us a sense of purpose. In that moment, we matter. We have something to offer. We were specifically seen and noticed as worthy.

So, when we're not chosen, we feel the opposite.

It's hard, in moments where someone else is chosen over us, to maintain the confidence that we still have value and worth. Just because it's not recognized in that specific moment doesn't mean that it doesn't exist.

The truth is that we have value in Jesus, and no person or rejection can diminish that.

The revelation that we were chosen by God before we were even born is such a freeing and life-changing truth. I won't lie; some days, it's still hard to believe. When I think about the places in my life where I have felt small, worthless, and unable to measure up, I can't imagine why God would choose me. It would be like someone choosing my artwork to be displayed in a museum. If you've ever seen my sad attempts at drawing even stick figures, you understand this. If I'm a complete stranger to you, and my analogy makes absolutely no sense because you've never witnessed my lack of ability in any sort of art, then make your own. Think of whatever area you are not naturally skilled in and picture yourself being honored in that area. It doesn't make sense. It would make us feel uncomfortable and insecure because it's not a deserved calling.

And that's the reality of how we can feel when we think about God choosing any of us. For so long, I couldn't wrap my head around this idea because I knew I didn't deserve to be called. My goodness, if you guys knew half of the demerits I've accumulated on my heavenly report card, it would ruin any credibility you may have given me.

And yet, that's the point.

God doesn't choose us because we deserve glorified recognition. He chooses us in our imperfection because *He* deserves the glory.

We are not chosen because we're good. We're chosen because He's good.

Let's look at God's track record.

We will start with the first person I hope to have a cup of coffee with in heaven, Moses. I love this guy, for real. I'm so excited to talk about him that my fingers are moving too quickly, and I just had to retype this sentence four times in order to correct the spelling.

The reason I love Moses so much is that I can identify with him. This may come as a shock to you, but my palms sweat profusely, and my heart beats like a jackhammer right before I have to give a presentation of any kind. The reason I decided to initially pursue a career to be on camera as a journalist is beyond me because my nerves were always prevalent as soon as the red recording light blinked on. No matter how prepared I felt, there was always an anxiety that came along with presenting or speaking in front of people. So, there's a deep secret of mine revealed to you. You're welcome.

Similarly, Moses felt unqualified to speak because he was "slow of speech and tongue" (Exodus 4:10). Although I don't have a physical condition that alters my speech, I do have an overwhelming fear that causes me to trip over words and forget the very message I had prepared. True story, y'all.

But God didn't look at Moses' inability to deliver fast messages equipped with fancy words and relatable puns. He was looking for a willing heart that He could use to show His glory.

Had Moses been qualified with a charismatic charm and a smooth tongue, he may have taken the glory for delivering the people of Israel from Pharaoh's grip. Because of his imperfection, there was only one person who could get the glory for the words that were spoken through him—and that was God.

> *The Lord said to him, "Who gives human beings*
> *their mouths? Who makes them deaf or mute? Who*
> *gives them sight or makes them blind? Is it not I, the*

Lord? Now go; I will help you speak and will teach
you what to say."

Exodus 4:11–12 (NIV)

I love that so much. Moses was nervous because he felt completely unqualified for what God had chosen for his assignment. In his worry, God comforts him by offering him the truth that he does not need to rely on his own strength but that God will be the One to strengthen and empower him to fulfill his purpose.

You may feel unqualified or unfit for the purpose that God has given you, but He specifically chose you for a reason.

God chose Moses and many others in the Bible because of one thing: their willing hearts.

As a lacrosse and soccer coach, my favorite players were the ones who came to practice with a determined attitude. They may not have been the most skilled or the most crafty players, but they were willing to learn, grow, and become stronger.

In the same way, God will help sharpen our tools and strengthen our abilities through His wisdom, guidance, and teaching. But if we reject this, He will choose someone else.

Let's look at King Saul.

Saul was the epitome of what the people wanted: handsome, strong, and a solid leader. He was fit to be the king, by the world's standards. He would've certainly had a blue checkmark next to his Instagram handle and a few million followers. He probably would have even landed the lead spot on *The Bachelor*.

But, in his pride, he rejected God. He thought he was good enough without Him and decided that his own strength would bring him through.

So, God chose David.

David—a shepherd boy. David—a young boy who wasn't even thought of as a contender to be king by his own father. David—the one that was overlooked by human standards but chosen by God because of his servant's heart.

Wow.

> *The Lord does not look at the things people look at.*
> *People look at the outward appearance, but the Lord*
> *looks at the heart.*
>
> 1 Samuel 16:7 (NIV)

God doesn't choose us by the standards of the world. He chooses us based on our heart's willingness to serve Him.

David wasn't perfect by any means. He committed adultery and murder, and yet he was still chosen by God to be king over His people.

Moses' insecurity and, ironically, pride found him in a lot of trouble, but he was still chosen by God to lead one of the most powerful exploits in biblical history.

And we can't forget about Paul! Paul—the dude who was having Christians killed—was chosen by God to then write two-thirds of the New Testament and spread the Gospel all over the world!

There are so many other examples, but I'll encourage you to go read about the people that God chose to include in the Bible because their stories are incredibly illustrative of God's mercy and power.

We, too, can offer the world a canvas that portrays how amazing, mighty, and capable our God is. While we can never offer

God our perfection, we can offer Him our hearts, and with that, there is nothing He can't do with our lives.

Okay, I totally understand if this is disheartening, though. When I began to discover how God could use me, I was also accepting that I must have some pretty serious faults because He uses the unexpected, the foolish, the last round picks, the uneducated, the unqualified. Should I just accept that and label myself as absolutely useless?

The short answer is no. But for a while, I fixated on this notion that God must be using me because I am an absolute failure when, in reality, He also planted strengths in me to fulfill my calling.

Yes, we have weaknesses. But we also have strengths. Our weaknesses are present so that we rely on God, and we can use our life for His glory, but our strengths are meant to glorify Him as well.

I sure can talk. It's definitely a strength of mine. But I also get incredibly nervous before I talk and let my anxiety consume my confidence. This is a weakness. So, I have the skills needed to live out my purpose, but I simultaneously need to consistently rely on God to help me do so. His power is made perfect in my weakness.

There are going to be moments where you feel incompetent and insecure, but those are the moments when God shows His mighty power best.

God's track record shows that He chooses imperfect people in order to portray His perfection.

I'm always so impressed when I see beautiful pieces of furniture contrasted with a "before" picture of its original, ragged state. Most people would take a look at the worn-out wood and jagged edges and immediately deem its forever home to be the local junkyard. Yet, someone saw potential in its broken state, took it

Set Apart, Not Aside

home, and remodeled it into something beautiful. You can still see some of the jagged edges, and there's evidence of its age, but that is what makes it so unique and breathtaking. And what talent it takes for that person to be able to do that!

Similarly, God isn't waiting for you to recycle yourself into a brand new version before He chooses you. He's not waiting for you to fix your broken pieces and smooth out your rough edges before He decides to use you. Just as that person decided to use that old piece of furniture and create something unique out of it, God chooses you in your ragged state too.

I'm sorry that I just compared you to a junkyard piece of furniture, but we can all feel that way at times, am I right?

We all get caught up in striving to be some perfect version of ourselves before asking God to use us because we're afraid that He won't accept us as we are. Yet, the Word tells us the complete opposite.

Over and over again, there are affirmations that we are chosen because of who He is, not by our own accolades.

If you are a breathing human being, you have a purpose. Do you want to know how I know this? God wouldn't have created you if you didn't.

Why would He waste His time creating someone He didn't care deeply about? He didn't create you simply to fill space. He created you to live out a specific purpose that He chose, specifically for you. When we choose to pursue that purpose, we have fulfillment and a manifested confidence that outweighs the opinions of the world. When we live our lives for His will, not our own, we admit that we can't do this alone. We are admitting that we need a Savior and that it is not our own strength that carries us through.

However, it's important to recognize that we are partners with God. He won't do everything for us, and we can't do everything on our own. Like I mentioned before, it's all about balance. We do what we can, in wisdom, and allow God to do what we can't, in His perfect strength. But the most important task we have is to choose God back.

Yes, God created a specific purpose for each person, but not all people will choose to follow that purpose. In fact, most people choose to follow their own desires and are living out a purpose that doesn't align with God's. That's why you will also see, over and over again, that we are chosen *in* Christ. We are only able to be used for a fulfilling and complete purpose if we admit that Jesus Christ is our Lord and Savior. If we don't, our lives aren't pointing to Him, which is why so many celebrities or people of great "power" seem to be the most unfulfilled. Their lifestyles and talents are chosen by the world yet are dismissive of the One who gave them the talents they possess. Unless they are using those gifts for the kingdom, they will always feel a void because they have rejected the only One who can make them whole.

When you accept Christ as your Savior, you are made blameless in God's sight. You are covered in the blood of Jesus, and your sins are washed away. You are able to stand before God because you have been made righteous through Jesus. In the same way, you are able to stand before God as a willing pawn, ready to complete the task He has predestined for you.

All you need is Jesus. And suddenly, you are given new hope and a new story. Suddenly, your eyes will open to the destiny that He has called you to, like never before.

Set Apart, Not Aside

*I pray that the eyes of your heart may be enlightened
in order that you may know the hope to which he has
called you, the riches of his glorious inheritance in his
holy people, and his incomparably great power for us
who believe.*

Ephesians 1:18–19 (NIV)

I don't want to disappoint you, but I have to say it: we were really all created to do the *same* exact thing—to share the Gospel.

It's really all of our calling to spread the good news of who Jesus is. That's why God created us. Now, before you throw this book down out of confusion and frustration because I *just* preached to you that you're all unique and God gave you each a specific purpose, hear me out.

We all have the same general calling, but we each have a specific subcategory to that calling. Some are called to teach the Word; others are called to teach drama class in public schools. Some are called to lead worship; others are called to work at the local radio station. Some are city-living financial planners, and others are tomato-growing farmers in the South. Wherever God has planted you, and whatever career or situation He has placed you in, He can use you to share about Jesus. And each place, path, and circle that God entrusts you with requires different skills, personalities, and experiences.

I want you to look at your own life for a moment. What is your job? Where do you live? Who are your friends? Who are your archenemies? What are your hobbies? What do you do every day?

Now, think about who you are for a second. What are your biggest personality traits? What comes easily to you? What do you love doing?

How do these things intersect? Can you see why God may have placed you where He did? Can you see why He gave you the specific traits that He has?

It's also important to note that your specific role in your calling may change. The general calling (sharing the Gospel) never will, but your specific role to live that out may. Let me explain.

At one point in my life, I was a student. The next, I was an aspiring television producer. In the next season, I was a coach and a student again. Then, I was a waitress and an aspiring teacher. Then, I was a restaurant manager and a babysitter. Now, as I write these words, I'm getting ready to pack up my New York life and move to North Carolina to pursue a career in full-time ministry as a social media manager.

Simultaneously during these seasons, I was an athlete, a daughter, a friend, a sister, a writer, and, most recently, a dog mom. My life is all over the place, and my resume is often confusing to most people, but I know that every experience I've had, and every place that I've been to, has helped me become the person I am today and has offered specific platforms for God to use me.

While my position, title, and location may change, who I am doesn't have to. I can be the same quirky girl with a New York-paced energy down in the South. I may stick out like a sore thumb, but God will use those traits that He has given me in some capacity.

So, don't be surprised if your situations change or if people come and go from your life. Don't discount your calling if you don't see its manifestation right away. Wherever He plants you, God will use it to help bloom you and others around you. There is a purpose to His planting, and there is a purpose to the type of person you are. God doesn't make mistakes—why do you think He did with you?

You are chosen to live a destined life that brings Him glory. It may not look like preaching to millions or traveling as a world missionary, but the love you show others and the mercy you are willing to extend will be an example of Jesus. The way you stand in hope when life gets tough is an illustration of faith. The way you offer a comforting hand to those around you in their time of need is a portrayal of God's compassionate nature. You are His hands and feet. And you were chosen to exemplify that to this world, wherever God has planted you.

How rad is that?

REFLECTION QUESTIONS

1. Why is it reassuring to know that God's purpose for our life is not determined by our successes/strengths?

2. How do you feel God can use your weaknesses right where you are?

3. Where has God planted you right now? Why do you think He chose that specific path for you?

4. How can you illustrate God's love to others right where you are this week?

5. Why is it fulfilling to know that you are chosen by God?

CHAPTER 7
FAIRYTALES GOT IT WRONG, AGAIN

And I pray that you, being rooted and established in love, may have power, together with all the Lord's holy people, to grasp how wide and long and high and deep is the love of Christ, and to know this love that surpasses knowledge—that you may be filled to the measure of all the fullness of God.

Ephesians 3:17b–19 (NIV)

Sorry to put Disney and Nicholas Sparks down again, but, man, did they get it wrong. Well, for their respective platforms of delivering happy, butterflies in your stomach, romantic endings, I guess they got it right. But as far as a realistic portrayal of what love truly is supposed to be, they got it so wrong.

The truth is, love is not conditional. It's not supposed to be based on your feelings and emotions and the fireworks that blast into the sky at the moment of your first kiss. Love is not something that you give or receive because it is deserved. In fact, love is just the opposite of that. Love is a choice, despite the other person's flaws, messiness, and quirks. It's a choice made with intentionality, even when the honeymoon stage ends and you are strangely aware of all of the annoying traits that your significant other didn't seem to have when you chose to pursue them. Love is choosing to sacrifice your selfish motives to care for someone else, even when your flesh fights it. Love is a choice. And it is unconditional.

For all other attributes of love and a live listen into any wedding ceremony, please see 1 Corinthians 13:1.

I can't sit here and explain to you what love actually is in its entirety because that would require a whole other novel and a few more. Also, with a bare left ring finger, it's obvious that I have some more studying to do and tests to pass before I'm qualified for that one.

But I do want to focus on the very truth that you *are* loved. And that love is not based on what you do, how you dress, how much you weigh, or what you choose to eat on a first date. That love is unconditional, and it will always exist, no matter what you do, whether you like it or not—which, how could you not?

If you're shaking your head in disbelief, unable to grasp how someone could love you no matter what, you're not alone. Although I've claimed this over my life, I still find myself trying to earn God's love by works. And I find myself doing it over and over again because I base His love off of the world's illustration of what that four-letter word is.

If I know one thing for certain, it's this: people will disappoint you. Their reliance on fickle feelings and selfish ways will undoubtedly leave you feeling unloved at many moments. Even the people who claim to love you endlessly will disappoint you. Even you will disappoint the ones who you claim to love with all of your heart. It's inevitable because we're human. And humans, as much as they yearn to love unconditionally, will always fight the flesh in offering that kind of love.

But there is one kind of love that will never, ever let you down. It's the kind of love that is unfathomable and breathtaking because it's based solely on His goodness and not our performance. And that's the love of God. God is love. It's His nature and everything that He is. He loves you more than you could fathom, and that's because He is more amazing, wondrous, and mighty than we can even imagine.

So, if you're having trouble understanding how a God, who created the Universe and everything in it, in His absolute perfection, sees you, in your messy ways and imperfect behavior, and still looks at you with loving eyes, then you're not alone. Because it truly is so incredible and hard to understand.

Choosing to believe that God loves us unconditionally takes faith. We can't wrap our heads around it, and it defies every societal view of what love should be, but God's Word says it's true, so we have to choose to believe it. And the more we choose to believe it, the more we will root that belief in our hearts. And the more rooted we are, the less we will be able to be destroyed by winds of human rejection and disappointment.

Remember fourteen-year-old Danielle? With her braces and dramatic breakup story? Remember how she was rooted in insecurity rather than the knowledge that she was deeply loved, just as she was? Well, fourteen-year-old Danielle was destroyed emotionally. And so was fifteen-, sixteen-, seventeen-, eighteen-, nineteen-, and on, and on year-old Danielle. The more she was disappointed by possible love interests, the more cynical she became. And the more cynical she became, the less hope she had and the less worth she felt in herself.

Although I still have my struggles with self-worth, I can confidently say that I am able to bounce back a lot quicker than I used to. Those self-pity parties don't stay long, and I can crawl out of those holes by standing on the truth that I am loved. No matter how I feel, who sees my worth, or what my life may look like: I am loved, just as I am. I don't need to lose ten pounds, post half-naked pictures of myself, or become less talkative to qualify myself to be loved. I am lovable just as I am: with my soccer thighs, dad-joke humor, fully-clothed pictures, and loud mouth.

I am fully loved on my bad days. You know, the ones where I react out of anger and get annoyed by everything? The ones where I snap easily or make poor decisions or act selfishly? I am loved every single day that I am on this earth because His love is not based on anything but the fact that He is love. That's just what He does and who He is. Nothing will make Him love me any more or any less than He does at this very moment.

And the same goes for you.

Although I reference romantic love here, I want to also hone in on platonic love. The same rejection that we face from potential love interests also exists within our friend circles. I cannot tell you how many times I've been disappointed by the people with whom I was supposed to be closest. Some of my very best, closest friends have left me feeling worthless. Their rejections of who I was could have been as simple as a negative statement that they made about my outfit or as large as a personal, vulnerable moment that they shared with others without my permission. In whatever capacity the hurt came, it came. And immediately, their actions fed my belief that there was something wrong with me.

There is a saying that goes like this: "Hurt people, hurt people." Sometimes, the conniving words spat at you are not intended to reveal your shortcomings but rather a derivative of an intent to hide someone else's. People who already feel hurt and rejected can often use putting others down as a means to make themselves feel better. And sometimes, these people truly do love you, deep down.

Of course, when words are exchanged or people are left out, it can certainly feel as though those people don't love us anymore. It can feel like our friends don't care about us or have a sudden deep hatred for all that we are. But in reality, I have found that they aren't acting intentionally, trying to make you feel worse. Maybe they're hurting pretty badly inside, or maybe they had a horrible day. Sometimes, we may never know, but it's important to remember not to take their harmful words or actions as truths that can keep us in a stronghold of defeat.

I'm not saying that we should just let others treat us any old way. There are certain boundaries to be made in certain situations, and it's imperative that you use wisdom on when to stay in a friendship and when to walk away. I do, however, want you to focus on the point that people cannot define you. They cannot hold your worth in their hands because they have too many fickle feelings to be able to do so.

Let me give you an example. My mom is probably the best human on this earth. There's really no debate here. She is like a walking, talking angel. Have there been times where my actions towards her and my words spewed her way made her feel less than that? Absolutely. I have had some moments that I'm not too proud of that were birthed from hurt and emotional exhaustion that certainly could have planted thoughts in my mom's head that she wasn't a good role model or that she lacked in some area of parenting. However, the truth is I love my mom to death, and I really do mean it when I say I hope I am even half of the godly woman, wife, and mom she is someday. I pray that my own selfish actions and words never made her feel anything less than incredible because that's truly who she is.

So, when you experience hurtful words or behaviors from those who are closest to you, please don't label yourself as "unlovable." Please don't automatically fall into a pit of self-despair that begs to directly correlate your worth with a measure of how much love you are receiving from those around you. Because "love" doesn't always look like a night under the stars on the state fair's Ferris wheel, or a grand gesture that makes your heart melt, or a beautiful bouquet of flowers delivered to your work. And even if you were to never receive love from any human on this planet during your life, you still wouldn't be able to label yourself as unlovable because God's Word says you are loved.

So, you, my friend, are loved. Whether you see it, deserve it, or feel it: you are loved. Say it out loud: "I am loved." Say it ten times in a row. Say it one hundred times if you're feeling crazy. Write it with lipstick on your mirror. Etch it with a pen on an index card and stick it in the visor of your car. Make it your phone background.

However you want to remind yourself, please intentionally do so because God loves you right where you are, regardless of if you deserve it or not. And there is nothing that can separate you from that unfathomable type of love.

It's important to cling to this truth because it will serve as a foundation for the filter that your thoughts run through. The next time you are faced with disappointment, rejection, or hurt, I pray that you won't let detrimental lies that you are unloved keep you in a place of bitterness or depression. I pray that you will fill any void with the truth that you are immensely loved by your Heavenly Father, who looks at you with adoration, regardless of how the world looks at you.

When you fill yourself with that truth, you will begin to feel the fullness of God because He is able to fill you with His comfort. When you are filled with the love of Christ, you are able to love others with more compassion, empathy, and patience because that's the way He loves us. The more we allow Christ in, the more we start to reflect His image. And the more we can focus on loving others, the less time we spend thinking about ourselves.

If you really think about it, self-pity is actually an illustration of pride. While it may seem like it is a complete contrast, staying in a place of despair caused by thoughts about our own image is incredibly egotistical because it suggests that we are in continuous thought about ourselves.

I know you're probably not my biggest fan after that statement, but it's a profound realization that has aided me in my growth in facing insecurity. The less I focus on myself, whether positive or negative, the less I have found myself staying in states of self-pity.

I'm not saying that spending time with your thoughts or yourself, in general, is a bad thing, and I'm not suggesting completely neglecting yourself. It's all about ratio and balance. When we conflate *all* of our thoughts to be about ourselves, that's when the danger ensues.

Do you see how the simple yet immensely complex word "love" can cause such strife in our life? Do you see how simply changing our perception can release so much freedom in our lives?

Listen, you can still enjoy a good Nicholas Sparks' film and soak in the romantic moments of life, but remember to intentionally choose to love yourself and others around you, even if you don't feel the butterflies anymore. And never, ever convince yourself of the lie that you are unloved. You are loved. And you can access that love to fill whatever void you need to, no matter where you are or what you've done. I promise. Ephesians 3:17b–19: read it. Study it. And I pray that you grasp it.

REFLECTION QUESTIONS

1. What has your idea of "love" been? Does that align with what God's definition of love is?

2. How can you learn not to take rejection personally?

3. What steps can you take to remind yourself that God loves you, unattached to what you do or how you feel?

4. How does loving others decrease your chances of falling into a depression fueled by self-pity?

CHAPTER 8
YOU ARE WHAT YOU THINK YOU ARE

For as he thinks in his heart, so is he.

Proverbs 23:7 (NLV)

As it has probably become increasingly obvious by this point in the book, the initiation behind low self-esteem begins within our minds. Our thoughts on ourselves, God, and the world around us directly influence how we feel and act. Everything that we do or say begins with a thought. And when that thought is negative or rooted in a lie, it can hinder us from accessing all that God intends to do in and through us.

You see, thoughts that are detrimental to us don't always have to feel like bad thoughts. For example, thoughts of pride quite often feel good to us. A thought that puts someone else down and simultaneously raises us up can feel good in our mind, but it hinders us from humbly walking out our God-given purpose. I may be entertaining thoughts that make me feel like the king of the world without realizing that I am also making someone whom I dearly love feel as though they were worthless.

The devil loves to use our mind as a ground to plant his most vicious attacks against us. He does this because he's smarter than you think. I hate to give the dude credit, but he knows what he's doing when it comes to strategic attacks. He knows that if he can control our thought process, he can also produce negative reactions that are intended to keep our eyes off of Jesus and our minds off of understanding who we fully are in Christ. If he can keep us from focusing on that, he can diminish the influence we will have for the kingdom of God. And that is exactly what he wants.

The thing is, our thoughts don't always align with who we are or what our values are. I'll give you a prime example.

One time, my lovely fur child, Molly Rue, would not sit still during a long car ride. She was drooling all over the place, and her inability to relax caused me to lose focus on the road several times. After about ten minutes of whining, constant attempts to climb in my lap as I drove, and showers of dog saliva, I had enough. A thought crept into my mind that made me question if I was even saved: *What if I just pulled over right now and left her there?*

Please don't call it animal cruelty; I cry if I have to reprimand this dog vocally. So, relax. And if you are in utter shock and disappointment right now, you are probably so holy and put together that you don't even need this book. The point I'm trying to make here is that this thought was clearly not one that I intended to act on or one that aligns with my values at all. In fact, it's the exact opposite. Nevertheless, it found itself in my mind, and I had a choice with what I was going to do with that thought.

> *We demolish arguments and every pretension that sets itself up against the knowledge of God, and we take captive every thought to make it obedient to Christ.*
>
> 2 Corinthians 10:5 (NIV)

This verse illustrates the truth that we can wrestle with thoughts that aren't in line with what we believe. If we didn't deal with thoughts that are in contrast to who we are, the Word wouldn't call us to action. We have to intentionally take each thought that enters our little minds and "make it obedient to Christ." This means we should match every thought we have to the Word of God. Our filter is the Bible. If that thought is in alignment with what is written in the Word, then you keep that thought as it is. If it is not, you combat it with the truth. It's a process, and it takes work, but it is imperative to emotional and mental healing.

My heinous thought about completely giving up on my dog was one birthed from intense anger, frustration, and annoyance. And yes, I repented hard on that one, okay? When emotions are high, we can allow skewed thoughts to reign in our minds. The process of deciding which thoughts we should focus on and which we should demolish is one that requires careful, steadfast attention. Usually, heightened emotion completely hinders our ability to be careful or steadfast.

In the same way, we have to pay attention to the thoughts we think about ourselves. Once you let one lie penetrate your mind, the domino effect begins, and it opens a door for more to spiral off of it. That's how I found myself wanting to end my life at the age of twenty-one.

It started with a thought of insecurity, a thought that was so small and seemingly insignificant. It didn't make a boisterous entrance or claim a large space in my head, initially. It whispered the thought that I was ugly, which then led to the thought that I would never find love. That then led to the thought that I was unworthy, and suddenly, I felt every shame of my shortcomings in one wave—a tsunami of guilt that stifled my ability to see any purpose in my life. It was a thick, dense cloud that filled every part of my body, and I found myself sitting on the hardwood floor of a college dorm, wondering if I would always have these encounters with an aching pain that, ironically, led to complete numbness. Another thought that plagued my mind was in the form of a question: "Will it always be this way?"

Thankfully, my attempt wasn't successful, and I was able to get the help I needed at that point in my life. Although I had acted on those thoughts in that specific moment, it wasn't the first time I allowed my mind to spiral to that point. There were many times before that, I just didn't know how to articulate them, and I didn't know how to act on them. Quite frankly, they scared me. But I felt them. They were present. And now I see why.

If I had been rooted in God's truth back then, I would have combatted the first whisper with Psalm 139. I would have filtered that thought out and focused on who God says I am. I would have shifted my attention to the truth of Jeremiah 29:11—that God has a beautiful plan for my life. I could have intentionally combatted the negative spiral with the truth of Ephesians 2:8–9—that I am forgiven not because of what I've done but because of who God is. I would have remembered that grace is a free gift, and I cannot earn it anyways. I could have broken the bondage of shame over my mind and clung to the promise of hope that Jesus offers every single one of us through His blood.

I'm not mad at my younger self for not knowing that I had this weapon against these thoughts, but I'm sad for her. If she had known that they were all lies filling her mind, she might have skipped the nights full of the strongest heartache she had ever felt. And this is exactly why I'm sharing this with all of you for the very first time. If you can learn from my season of hurt, please do. There is freedom to be found before you get to that dark place. And I pray that you find it sooner than I did.

There is such power in speaking scripture against our thoughts. Because I have a pretty horrible memory, I have become a crazy sticky note lady. If you came over to my apartment, you would see cards and notes with scriptures and truths on them scattered on my walls. These serve as reminders of my intention to speak over my mind daily. This is not a one-and-done kind of deal. The devil doesn't stop because you fought back once. I don't say that to scare you, but I say it to remind you that true strength comes in repetition. That's why you don't get a six-pack after doing one crunch. Although, that would be really nice, wouldn't it?

The devil uses thoughts of insecurity to keep us in a place where we cannot have influence. Sometimes, these thoughts are huge waves that consume everything we are. But most of the time, they are little whispers that gently nudge us away from stepping into what God has called us to be.

There was this super cool girl who seemed to be my age that started going to my church a little while back. I was so intimidated by her in so many ways. She was pretty, had a confident aura about her, and was clearly rooted in her faith. Every time I saw her, I wanted to approach her to try and be friends, but a whisper always came that suggested that I wasn't worthy of being in her presence. It was a different lie each time, and they were so small that I could barely feel the weight of them, but they were still enough to keep me from pursuing a friendship with this girl.

A few years later, I finally mustered up the courage to start chatting with her. It took everything in me to do that, and I held my breath right before approaching her, but I'm so beyond thankful that I did because now she happens to be one of my best friends and one of the best people in my life. I had been praying for a friend who was rooted in Christ and someone that could help strengthen my faith. God had answered my prayer, but the devil's lies kept me from accessing that blessing. He kept me focused on my lack, which made me feel unworthy, which ultimately kept me from someone who I could have really used in my life back then. Of course, I'm beyond grateful that we are friends now, but I kick myself for ever letting myself feel so small.

Now that I know her, she is totally just as cool and pretty and awesome as I imagined her to be. But those truths about her didn't have anything to do with the lies that I was being fed about myself. She has so much more wisdom than I do, but that is such an asset to me because she has helped me grow so much in the Lord, and I am forever grateful for that. The devil saw that as a hindrance to his plan of keeping me from any sort of growth, so of course, he did his best to stop the relationship from ever forming. Well, the joke's on you, buster.

Do you see how we do this? We should celebrate other people's strengths and learn from them, not compare ourselves and negate our own potential. We're all in different areas of life, and we all have different experiences. Where we are weak, someone else may be strong. But simultaneously, we are strong where others are weak. This is why we need fellowship and relationships. God created us differently for this reason. How boring would it be if everyone knew everything, and everyone was good at everything? In fact, you wouldn't have an appreciation for what "good" was if there was nothing to compare it to.

The reason I get goosebumps when I hear an amazing singer is because I've heard my own poor attempt at singing, which sounds eerily similar to nails on a chalkboard. There is a clear distinction between horrible pitch and angelic voices because I've heard the contrast in them. If everyone were Whitney Houston, there would be less appreciation for good singing. And with less appreciation would come less emotional response, which would diminish the opportunity for those moments that take your breath away and leave you in awe. How boring of a world would that be?

So, someone may be different than you or better than you in certain areas, but that doesn't give your mind the permission to take that thought and turn it into a truth that you are less worthy than them. Maybe you are less artistic than they are, but you are not less important. Maybe your hair is not as luscious as theirs, but that does not mean that you weren't created with the same amount of intentional attention and detail. Maybe they are a better speaker than you, but that does not mean that you don't have a calling in your life.

When we get wrapped up in the thoughts of comparison, we are giving the devil permission to take us down a rabbit hole fueled by insecurity, which takes the focus off of the truth that we have a unique purpose in our life that God fully intends to fulfill.

I became so consumed by thoughts of envy that I felt unworthy to be in another girl's presence. That then led to me thinking that she was going to absolutely hate me because I wasn't worthy of being around her. Now that I know her, I can laugh at the absurdity of that thought because this girl is actually the sweetest human being alive and would hang out with anyone who had a pulse. She is still as cool and pretty and awesome as I thought she was, but she is not a judgmental Regina George figure who wouldn't dare be caught in my presence like my mind tried to convince me she was. All of that nonsense and years wasted without my best friend in my life simply because of one thought. Isn't that crazy?

I wish I could say that navigating our thoughts is an easy task or a one-and-done conquering process. While our ability to flush out the negative thoughts may get stronger, those thoughts never learn that our mind is unwanted territory. Like someone who can never seem to read the room, negative thoughts keep coming back for more, even when they're continuously asked to leave. But don't worry because the better you get at fighting them, the easier they become to ward off. Awareness and preparation are key.

So, first and foremost, open your Bible, or your Bible app, or Google, and get some scriptures into your playbook. I can't tell you which ones you'll specifically need because the enemy knows our specific weak points, but I can encourage you to look up those areas that you seem to struggle with the most and find the verses that are relative to it. Otherwise, it would be like taking a frying pan to a battlefield, which only works for Rapunzel.

Now, if you're like me, memorization is a tough skill to master. So, don't beat yourself up if you can't recite the entire New Testament by next Tuesday. I would try to memorize one or two scriptures that resonate with you most and offer you the most peace in quick situations when you say them aloud. For other moments, I turn to my favorite tactic of learning scripture: sticking them on my walls.

When I was little, it was rare that the walls of our house didn't have at least three index cards with scriptures written on them. My mom was a crazy index card lady who wanted you to get a look at the Bible wherever you went. Now, as a young adult, I realize that she was posting them as reminders for herself and easy, accessible weapons against the devil's attacks all day long. I may have made fun of her before I understood, but now, twenty years later, I find myself marking my walls at home and at work with scriptures on post-it notes, index cards, and scrap paper.

Set Apart, Not Aside

Now, when I find those negative thoughts attempting to contradict the very truth of what God's Word says about me, I can quickly find something to combat them with. There is power in speaking Scripture aloud. That's why it's referred to as a "double-edged sword." It's a tool to attack and defend against the enemy.

So, the next time a thought comes into your head suggesting that you have no purpose, shout Psalm 139 and Jeremiah 1:5 back at it. The next time you are dealing with intense shame and guilt, remind yourself of Ephesians 2:8–10. I could go on and on, but this is a personal journey that you should go on for yourself.

The more you read the Word, the more you will start to grasp who you are because it's in those pages that you will see who He is. And you cannot fully understand your own identity until you know about the One who created you.

REFLECTION QUESTIONS

1. What thoughts have you been thinking about yourself?

2. Do those thoughts agree with what you read in the Bible?

3. What should you do when a negative thought comes into your mind?

4. What are a few scriptures that you can write out to help fight against bad thoughts?

5. Bonus: Write them out and stick them where you'll see them most.

CHAPTER 9
HEY MILLENNIALS, STOP "SOUL-SEARCHING"

In Him we were also chosen, having been predestined according to the plan of Him who works out everything in conformity with the purpose of His will, in order that we, who were the first to put our hope in Christ, might be for the praise of His glory.

Ephesians 1:11–12 (NIV)

So, the question now becomes: how do we understand our true identity? How can we fully understand all that our soul is made of and what makes up the inner core of who we are as a human?

I'm just going to be real honest with you right now; the answer to this may disappoint you because you've been taught that all of the answers you need for life can be found if you just look within yourself. Well, this is partially true, but they can only be found if you're looking at Jesus living inside of you. If you're just looking for the answers from yourself, you'll always feel a void.

Let me explain further.

I am writing this book right now. And you will read its words and get what you need from it, but you will never cherish it the way I will unless you take the time to ask me about every step of its creative process and why I decided to publish it for the world—or just my mom and her friends—to see.

The words you are reading derive from twenty-six years of experience birthed from heartbreak, failures, disappointments, joyful moments, mountaintops, and mundane moments. They are words that I decided to bring forth because I knew they would serve a purpose, and they mean so much to me because they're personal. While you may resonate with bits and pieces of this book, I think you would feel its weight much deeper if you understood me as the author. This is why I've tried to offer some personal anecdotes to give you some insight into the quirky, caffeinated chick with a messy bun typing these words.

Every time I see a piece of art, I'm not usually intrigued. Because I'm so artistically challenged, the only time I can truly understand what I'm looking at is when there's an accompanying documentary explaining the artist's thoughts behind why they created it. Then, I see the painting differently. Then, I can feel the emotion in it and understand its purpose.

Is it coming together now? You can't fully understand a creation until you understand the intention of its creator. This is why you can only find your true purpose and worth in the One who created you.

Yet, society has deemed the latest trend to be "finding yourself." For real—I can't scroll on any social media feed without seeing some sort of post about taking a journey to "find out who you truly are," as if a weekend at some retreat in the middle of nowhere is supposed to suddenly reveal everything you need to know about this soul that lives inside of your body.

Again, I'm not against spending intentional time developing and working on yourself. In fact, if I were, I wouldn't be writing this book, with its entire purpose being to help you discover your identity...but let me clarify this: I am against trying to figure out who you are without God at the center.

When God created us, He created us in His image. While we can't fully fathom and understand who God truly is, we can certainly study His attributes and learn more about why we are wired the way we are. He also created us with a specific purpose, and unless we decide to live for that will and not our own, we will always feel a gap in our souls that we will long to fill. And that is where the cyclical frenzy of searching begins. You can search all you want, but until you realize that your soul can only be completely full in Jesus, you will feel like something is missing.

My favorite drink to have by my side during any sports game was Gatorade. Cool Blue, to be exact. Bonus points if it was in one of those tall, squeezy bottles, or whatever they're called. When I would run to the sidelines, parched and looking for something to quench my thirst, I would find immediate solace in a cold, refreshing Gatorade. Yet, without fail, five minutes after that heavenly sip, my mouth would feel even more like a desert than it initially had. The truth is, as great as it tastes, Gatorade actually contains a boatload of sugar, which causes even more dehydration. My body didn't need sugar to replenish it: it needed water.

How many of us are running to Gatorade bottles of the world rather than giving our body the water that it truly needs—a relationship with Jesus? A weekend yoga retreat may be satisfactory for a moment, but when the workweek hits on Monday, do you still feel replenished? Did your sudden self-revelation that you have a passion for meditation act as a soul discovery for a moment? Sure, this may be a discovery about you, but it is not one that defines you. It is a sip of a refreshing Cool Blue Gatorade, but it is not the essential intake of water that will sustain you for far longer.

Let me put it to you this way. I have done some soul-searching in my own life. Since this phenomenon is practically plastered on social media, etched in school curriculums, and preached through movies and TV shows, it was inevitable that I would attribute my own lack of self-worth to a lack of self-discovery. This is a partially true statement. The problem was that I was forgetting to discover God's purpose for my life as the foundation.

Now, I bet I know your next question: "What is God's purpose for my life?" Excellent question. Personally, I'm not entirely sure what my purpose looks like, but I know that we are here to show people who Jesus is. How do I know this? Just read Ephesians. It's the book that completely transformed my view of not only who God is but also why He created me, and you, and everyone else.

We are here to represent His glory, and it is going to look different for each of us.

Recently, I got a dream opportunity to work for a church that I never even thought I'd have the privilege to attend, let alone work for. However, taking the job would mean packing up my life in New York and moving to a new state while simultaneously giving up on obtaining my master's degree in education. It would be a huge decision, and anxious thoughts kept me awake for forty-eight straight hours as I tried to decide which path God was trying to point me towards. I didn't have peace right away because I was so fixated on the possibilities of both and worried that I would get the decision wrong.

I was annoyed because I wanted God to come down from heaven and sit on my bed and tell me exactly what He wanted me to do. I wanted Him to give me red flags on one path and green arrows on the other.

When I was waiting for the answer to whether or not I got the job at this church, my stomach constantly felt like it had just eaten something expired. The bags under my eyes illustrated the very lack of sleep my body got over the span of three days between the interview and the result. I was a wreck. I hated not knowing, but I think more than anything, I was afraid of a reply of "Congratulations, you got the job!" because it would mean having to make a decision. And I am *not* a good decision-maker. For real. Hence, the constant anxiety.

But, Galatians 5:16–17 (NIV) reveals the source of this struggle, "So I say, walk by the Spirit, and you will not gratify the desires of the flesh. For the flesh desires what is contrary to the Spirit, and the Spirit what is contrary to the flesh. They are in conflict with each other, so that you are not to do whatever you want."

So, if you're stuck in this worrisome rut where you can't figure out if your life is on track with what God wants for you, spend time with Him and ask Him. If you're not in a place that is beneficial for you, He'll let you know. And I'm not talking about surface-level feelings here. You may be in a job that you really don't love, but God is using you in a big way there. Something, deep down, will let you know. It's the little nudge in your gut telling you that you need to stay or leave. It's the small whisper that's settled in your soul after the noise of reactive emotion and other people's opinions die out. It's the voice of the Holy Spirit. But you can only hear it when you get in a quiet place, free from the distractions of people, media, and just life in general. It's a deep knowing, not a feeling. This is the contrast between the flesh and the Spirit.

That's how I knew I was about to tell everyone in New York that I was out. As much as I loved the place I called home for twenty-six years, and as much as my heart wanted to pursue teaching, there was something in me that just knew that I had to pack my bags and leave it all behind for something greater that God wanted to do.

Now, if I had done it the world's way and tried to dig deep within myself for the answer, leaving God out of the equation, I might have stayed right where I was. I might have wrestled with the fact that I do love kids, and my education classes always sparked a joy in me that ceased to exist in any of my other college classes.

I might have focused on the part of me that is extremely family-oriented and stayed behind just to be close to them. Maybe, the part of my soul that is in love with the Hudson Valley fall foliage would have beckoned me to stay simply for the three months of the year that offered an environment painted with gold, orange, pink, and emerald streaks.

But these bits of my soul aren't the ones that are the most important. Just because these things happen to make my heart jump a little faster than normal doesn't mean that they are reflective of where I'm supposed to be. They are important to notice, but not as an end-all-be-all to following God's purpose.

Instead, when I have these moments where I can feel my soul stirring at a faster pace, I thank God for the little moments that help me enjoy my time on earth. How horrible would it be if nothing excited you or made you feel a little more alive than usual? God isn't some meanie pants who doesn't want you to enjoy life. He aligned your heart with little joys that can be found in everyday life so that you would have these moments. And they're

Set Apart, Not Aside

going to differ from person to person. But they are not your identity.

I am not just identified as a basic White girl because I could live in a coffee shop, sipping a pumpkin spice latte in an oversized flannel. I am a child of God who happens to like those things. They are part of my identity, but they do not make up the foundation of my identity. I'm thankful that God gave me these little joys in life, and if He has hidden them in the nooks of life for twenty-six years now, I am confident that He will continue to do that, wherever I may be.

Pay attention to the things you love, and make sure you embrace them to help you enjoy your life. But don't look for life's deepest answers in those things. Sadly, the bottom of an oat-milk latte with cinnamon powder sprinkled on top won't reveal wisdom, but if I'm seeking God while sipping on one, He will do that for me.

Again, I want to stress that if you are showing others around you who Jesus is by loving them and extending grace to them, you are living your purpose. If you are seeking God and even stressed, wondering if you are living in His will, you are definitely living your purpose. God asked us to do two things above all: love Him and love people. Ask God where He wants you to do that, and make sure you listen. He'll place you where He needs you to be. And you just might be surprised with where He can use you.

REFLECTION QUESTIONS

1. What are some things that spark your soul? How can you see those as things to enjoy, not be defined by?

2. Where is God using you right now? Are you loving the people around you and showing them Jesus?

3. How are you taking the time to listen to the Holy Spirit? What does your quiet time look like?

CHAPTER 10
EMBRACE YOUR INNER WEIRDO

Now if the foot should say, "Because I am not a hand, I do not belong to the body," it would not for that reason stop being part of the body. And if the ear should say, "Because I am not an eye, I do not belong to the body," it would not for that reason stop being part of the body. If the whole body were an eye, where would the sense of hearing be? If the whole body were an ear, where would the sense of smell be? But in fact God has placed the parts in the body, every one of them, just as he wanted them to be. If they were all one part, where would the body be? As it is, there are many parts, but one body.

1 Corinthians 12:15–20 (NIV)

When I was in college, I had to take a class that solely focused on creating a resume. My professor spent hours explaining the importance of creating a unique, vibrant template in order to stand out to potential employers. You'd want to keep it professional, of course. But some part of the page should be enticing enough to catch the eye of the lucky individual tasked with looking through hundreds and hundreds of one-page autobiographies. Countless

8.5 x 11 snapshots illustrating entire lives would come across their desk. How would we ensure that our piece of paper wouldn't end up in the trash pile after a five-second glance over? We have to make ourselves shine.

But don't stray too far from Times New Roman, and don't you dare let your achievements spill onto a second page. If you even think about adding samples of your creative work, you might as well get ready to stay unemployed for the rest of your life. Pizazz that page, but only with clear-cut fonts and big words that illuminate your strengths. You probably shouldn't offer a glimpse into your personality. Yikes, that would be a done deal.

That's society, isn't it? They encourage you to stand out, be yourself, march to your own tune! Oh, but don't wear your jeans like that, and don't you even think about getting that haircut. I wouldn't talk about those topics, and you should probably keep that odd hobby of yours a secret. Make sure you stack your free time with lots and lots of extracurriculars, but only the ones that are socially acceptable. Be unique, but only to the extent that you are exactly the same as everyone else.

No wonder we're all mentally and emotionally drained by the time we reach our twenties.

Here's the thing: my resume is probably never going to have some sort of intellectual achievement on it. It will probably never boast a scientific discovery that I somehow was a part of. I say "probably" because God can do anything, and who the heck knows? I don't want to limit the guy. But seriously, I am just not wired that way.

And that's okay. We weren't created to be all things. God gave us each a specific part in His kingdom, and He didn't intend for you to excel at every single thing. If you're not super talented in some areas, give yourself a break. That's probably not your calling.

I'm not saying that you need to be perfect or incredibly qualified in an area for God to use you, but pay attention to your strengths. There's a reason God gave you some natural abilities that others may not have.

How would God be able to use people in a hospital if everyone were built like me? I practically faint at the mention of blood, so we know that is not my calling. But I have friends who are incredible nurses and can somehow stick needles in people without blinking an eye. Truly incredible. However, they can't understand how I light up around kids, how I can talk to a complete stranger about seemingly nothing, or how I was the only person in my English classes who didn't groan at writing assignments.

We are built differently on purpose. There are so many places and environments that Jesus needs to be represented in, and we can't do that if we're not specifically designed for where we are.

I love that scripture in 1 Corinthians 12 that talks about the different parts of the body. Each part of our body is essential to the entire function, but they also each have unique functions. How annoying and overwhelming would it be if our legs, arms, and ears also had thoughts? Imagine having to make a decision and conversing with every part of your body for the answer? It's hard enough with just the mind producing those thoughts.

Each part of the body is essential in its own way, and when any is broken or missing, it becomes rather evident how crucial their role is. If you've ever had an injury, you know exactly what I mean. I jammed my pinky last week, and it made me realize how much I used my pinky in everyday activities. So, even if you feel like a pinky finger that is seemingly small and insignificant, your role is more important than you think.

You were called to a specific place to play a unique role that God tailored you for. When you start believing that, you can look past your weaknesses and trust that God has chosen you to be right where you are in this very moment. It's no mistake that you are in the position you are in. It's no mistake that you are in the environment you're in right now. It's no mistake, but God knew you'd be there, and He designed you to be able to function there. How incredible is that?

In fact, this can help us understand *why* we are the way we are.

If you've known me for more than five minutes, you're well aware that I have this special ability to strike up a conversation with even a wall. This past week, I've made four new friends in the new little town that I live in. They are all over the age of sixty-five, but I get so excited when I pass them on my daily walks. You'd be amazed at the information I muster up from the various thirty-second interactions we share from opposite sides of the road.

I know one had a dog named Molly as well, another loves the library, one has a niece who is visiting for the weekend, and another just had to put her furry friend down at the vet. I feel like the star of a Hallmark movie, minus the epic love story.

One common thread makes up the fabric of my new neighborhood friends: they are all always alone. Now, I'm not assuming that they're lonely or that they feel alone, but rather stating the matter of fact about their physical state when they walk. They are always by themselves.

I don't know if that means that they have no family waiting for them to return from their venture or if they have no coffee dates lined up with their friends from book club. I don't know how many friends they have on Facebook or if they even have social media, but I do know that God put them in my walking path for a reason.

I also know that he gave me an outgoing persona for a reason. And perhaps my seemingly natural decision to simply smile, wave, and say hello to these specific people during their solitary walks offered them a sense of companionship. Perhaps my friendly demeanor offered a glimpse of God's love and warmth that they have never experienced before or have been searching for. Perhaps one smile offered the notion that they were worth being noticed, and that was just the thing they needed to feel that day.

Now, I don't think that I'm this Miss America pageant contestant who is changing lives and offering world peace just because I know how to smile. I'm well aware that these interactions are not always life transformative or breathtaking moments. However, I'm certain that they are always spiritually divine.

I'm certain that God put those specific people in my walking path for a reason. I'm sure that God knew exactly what their hearts needed because it seems to be similar to the very ache, yearning for human companionship, and genuine interaction that mine has been feeling lately. God uses even the simplest of moments to reveal glimpses of His loving nature.

If I had a shyer persona, I'm not sure that I would've had the same interactions with my new friends. After all, I had to initiate each greeting. If I wasn't so inquisitive, I wouldn't have transitioned the initial meeting into an in-depth conversation, provoking meaningful dialogue. If I were anything but my curious, outgoing self, I might have passed by these folks and missed a divine opportunity to let God move in whatever way He intended to.

Maybe you're more on the quiet side, and God has put people in your life who find solitude in your presence. Perhaps He has given you a job that allows you to bring a calming effect on those around you, offering a glimpse of His peace. Maybe He has placed people in your life who need someone to simply listen, and you offer an uninterrupted ear to hear the pains that plague their hearts.

Let me tell you something. I am always trying so hard to shut my mouth when people talk to me. My goodness, do you know how hard it is to keep myself from interjecting some sort of answer, opinion, or anecdote into someone's conversation? It is truly a gift from God to be able to simply listen, and I'm working on that one myself.

But the point I'm getting at here is that you are made exactly how God wants you to be because there are so many different places and people that need to experience His presence, and it takes a plethora of personalities to reach each one.

God knew exactly where He would put you when He formed you. He made you the way that you are so that you would maximize your calling. However, it's important to recognize that we should always refine our character to look more like Jesus.

My big mouth can get me in a lot of trouble if I'm using it to spew anger or hate or simply seeking attention with it. My high energy helped get me a few reprimands in school (I know, I know, let's all gasp together), a lot of extra push-ups at practices, and even a few stern words from my father. The problem wasn't that I was talkative and bubbly—it was that I was using these gifts in the wrong way or at the wrong time.

I don't know what specific traits God has knitted into your being, but I know that we are created in His image, so our behaviors should be reflective of His. This is why it's not okay to justify anger by saying that God made you an angry person. It's not okay to justify pride by claiming it as a personality trait. We all have areas that we struggle with, but that doesn't mean that God made you that way.

Set Apart, Not Aside

He will, however, allow us to discover these weaknesses so that we humble ourselves and continuously seek God for strength. This is where we have to make the careful distinction between recognizing our weaknesses and making excuses for them. If you want to claim who you are in Christ, you have to understand that any piece of your identity that is in opposition to His character can't simply be accepted as a weakness. It has to be recognized and then dealt with. Isn't that so exciting? In the next chapter, we'll dive more into that. I know you can't wait, so gear up, and let's tackle it together.

REFLECTION QUESTIONS

1. What are some of your specific strengths?

2. Why do you think God has you in the place He does right now?

3. What function do you think you serve in the different environments that you're in?

4. How can you remind yourself that your role is vital to the kingdom?

CHAPTER 11
WE ARE NOT WORTHY: A NOBLE CHANT

But God demonstrates his own love for us in this:
While we were still sinners, Christ died for us.

Romans 5:8 (NIV)

One of my favorite things about the Bible is reading about all of the main characters that God chose to show His glory through. I love how they are presented. They aren't just glorified for their strengths; God is magnified through their struggles. The full scope of each character exhibits the very nature of God and offers hope for those of us who feel unqualified, less than, or unworthy.

Because the truth is, even in our strongest areas, we will still face some sort of insecurity. The devil doesn't want you to see yourself the way that God does, so he does everything in his power to knock you down a bit lower to stop you from fulfilling God's will for your life. Because if you're in God's will, you're producing fruit for the kingdom. And that's a big L for the devil right there.

I know I've expressed to you how much I love to talk. However, it shocks most people that I get extremely socially anxious and nervous in certain situations. It's actually pretty common for the devil to whisper constant doubt in my mind, spiraling a train of thoughts that suggest that everyone around me is judging and critiquing me.

It's why sometimes I can talk to a stranger, but other times I can't muster up the courage to go to a coffee shop alone in fear of what people might think of me. It's why I can post videos of me being a complete weirdo on my Instagram story and simultaneously fret that everyone now finds me annoying. It's the ironic and frustrating paradox that there is weakness even within my strength, and that leaves me feeling extra unworthy some days.

But the thing is, God never asked us for perfection. Sure, He gives us behaviors and rules to abide by, but they aren't a means of salvation. They aren't the key to heaven or the key to getting God to like you any more than He does at this moment. They are guidelines to protect us from living a life that is anything but full and whole.

God wasn't up in heaven waiting for everyone to get it together on earth so that He could finally give them the greatest gift He could offer through His Son. He sent Jesus to cover our sins because He is good, not because we are.

When you accept Jesus into your heart and truly love Him, you want to be better for Him. You want to live a life that is pleasing to Him out of love, not out of obligation. Well, at least, this is how it's intended to be. Instead, we have somehow morphed this idea of love into a vicious competition based on this notion of being "worthy of it." God doesn't love us because we are worthy of it; He loves us because He is worthy. This is why our whole society is backward.

As I type these very words, I'm sitting in one of my favorite places in the world. I'm actually pretty certain that my corner of heaven looks exactly like the Barnes & Noble I'm cozied up in with an oat milk latte from the Starbucks café inside.

Side note: I would like to ask why they proudly serve Starbucks but don't proudly take my Starbucks rewards here? Struggle city.

Anyways, here I sit, in pure bliss. And obviously, since I'm a total book nerd, I took a good half hour to peruse the book aisles before gluing my behind to the small table I'm currently writing from. While making my rounds, I caught something that caused me to physically shake my head and let out one of those disappointing laughs.

There was a shelf labeled "Religion" that held some of the books by incredible men and women of God that have helped strengthen my faith. Mostly, shout out to Lysa Terkeurst, Joyce Meyer, and Steven Furtick.

While I was looking at some of the new devotional journals, the aisle of books next to this one caught my eye. Its label read, "Self-Help." Most of the books promised keys to a better life and a better you! You hold every answer you need! You can solve all of your problems!

I mentioned that I let out a disappointing laugh, and if you're wondering what in the world that even is, I'll explain now. I laughed because of the happenstance that this shelf was right across the way from rows and rows of books that pointed to our problems only being able to be solved through help from Jesus. Essentially, we cannot fix ourselves by ourselves. We need Jesus. So, you pick up a book from that row, and you decide, "Yes! That's freeing. I can let God work out the things that I can't."

Then, you pick up a book from the aisle across the way. And now you're confused. Because you just admitted that you need Jesus, but you also have to figure this all out by yourself. Is your head spinning yet? No wonder this world is confused. This is where the disappointment factor came in.

I actually felt this sadness that people really believe that they have to strive to be better in everything to feel better. I felt sad that "success" is preached from text to be this tangible look that you have it all together, and you have to work harder to do so. No wonder anxiety consumes this generation. We have it all backward in contrast to how God intended it to be.

The world suggests that you are only lovable if you are worthy of it. It suggests that you need to fix the broken pieces of yourself or fix your weaknesses *before* you can live a fulfilled, happy life. But Jesus says, "Nah."

Jeremiah 1:5 (NIV) says, "Before I formed you in the womb I knew you." That means that God knew everything He was getting when He hit the "go" button on your life. He knew every mistake you would make, He knew every sin you would struggle with, and He knew every flaw you would fixate on. But He also knew every strength He would place in you. He knew every obstacle you would overcome, and He knew exactly how you would be before you even knew yourself. Nothing that you say or do is a surprise to God. He already knows.

If God made us all perfect beings, worthy of all of the love in the world, we wouldn't need Him. If God only loved us when we deserved it, we wouldn't stand in awe at how amazing He truly is. I don't think we can really fathom how amazing God is, and it's not because He loves us at our best, but because He loves us at our lowest.

God has shown me a small glimpse of this unconditional love through my own parents. I remember one of my lowest moments. I had messed up. And pretty darn badly. I'm not talking steal the last cookie from the cookie jar mess up; I'm talking big-time disappointment. I can vividly remember waking up the next day and leaving my phone on my nightstand without looking at it for a couple of hours. I couldn't muster up the courage to flip it over because I knew I would see at least 400 text messages and missed calls from my dad and probably a few more from my mom. I didn't want to face their disappointment. So, I hid in a dark room underneath a down blanket and heavy shame.

When I eventually faced my fears and picked up the phone to call them, their reaction surprised me. Yes, they were upset with my actions. But I was shocked to also simultaneously receive grace and love from them. I certainly wasn't worthy of it, but I'm their daughter, and they made it obvious that they love me—all of me—including the part of me that messes up big time.

If two human beings in their flesh can love me that way, how much more does a perfect God love me? God doesn't love you because you're perfect; He loves you because He is perfect. It has been at some of the times that I have felt least worthy that God has shown me His love in the greatest ways.

John 3:16 is one of the most powerful scriptures and sometimes loses its impact in the familiarity of it. I bet you could all recite it back to me right now, even if you aren't a believer.

> *For God so loved the world that He gave His one*
> *and only Son, that whoever believes in Him shall*
> *not perish but have eternal life.*
>
> John 3:16 (NIV)

Maybe you've said this verse a million times but never really felt the impact of it. I want to help shift your perspective today because this scripture is a citation for you so that you can attach "loved" to your permanent identity.

Before Jesus died on the cross, it was nearly impossible to live a life that would land you in heaven. If you messed up, you had to take some pretty intense steps and ask a priest who was considered worthy of being in God's presence to ask God for forgiveness for you. You couldn't just pause wherever you were and talk to God like you can now. You couldn't feel instantaneous freedom from sin just by asking for repentance.

God didn't want that for His people. He longed for a relationship with us. He didn't want us to live in bondage to our mistakes or continuously strive to be "good enough." So, out of love, He thought of you. Yes, you. He thought of your name and your life (remember, He knew you long before you were even born!), and He decided that He wanted you to live a life of freedom in Christ. So, He sent Jesus, His only Son, to die on the cross as the ultimate sacrifice so that you could have that life.

Now, I don't know what it's like to have a child yet. I don't know what that type of love is like, but I do know that if someone asked me to sacrifice my fur child, I would lose my mind. Sometimes, I have to intentionally think like that so I can attempt to understand even slightly the amount of love that God has for us.

You were not created to strive to earn God's love. When you love God, you want to grow to be more and more like Him, but the truth is, you will never reach perfection. If you could, you would be Jesus. But let me just break it to you now: you're not. So, there will always be some areas where we fall short in that God needs to work on. And if God is pointing out one of those areas to you right now, that should be even more of an indication of how much He loves you.

Hebrews 12:6 (NIV) says that God "disciplines the one He loves." If you're an athlete, you might understand it this way: when a good coach sees immense potential in you and they care about you, they want to see you grow. They will challenge you and gracefully push you while also celebrating where you're at. Sometimes, the challenging part can overshadow the celebration part, but it's still a sign of love. If they didn't care about you, they wouldn't take the time to help you grow in your weaknesses.

I remember feeling this way in soccer. My coach seemed to hold my attitude and behavior to a high standard. I remember wondering why it felt like she was harder on me than most of my teammates, especially since I wasn't even one of the top players.

And then, one of my friends said something that completely shifted my perspective: "She's hard on you because she cares about your growth." It was hard to hear and hard to endure, but I started to see her attention to my behavior as a compliment. She saw potential in who I was as a person and didn't want me to stay stagnant in my character. I learned countless lessons about leadership, humility, and work ethic from her, and while they were not always fun to go through, I will be forever grateful that she took the time to help develop those pieces of me.

Can I be real with y'all? If she didn't care enough to discipline me in those areas, I would still have a horrible attitude problem. I would still sulk after every mistake and self-sabotage any progress I had made. I would still have trouble coming under an authority that had a different perspective than me.

I'm not saying that I don't still struggle in these areas. But I have certainly grown a tremendous amount, and I am thankful that my coach invested the time to help recognize my weaknesses and challenge me to grow in them. It might not have felt good to me at the time, but it was a sign of love that helped produce fruit in my life.

Similarly, that weight you are feeling to outgrow some of the negative habits in your life is not a sign that God is mad at you;

it's quite the opposite. It's a sign that He loves you too much to let you stay in a place that isn't bearing fruit in your life.

You don't need to change your behavior to earn God's love; your behavior begins to change when you realize that God is molding you out of His love.

When you start to grasp that God's love is independent of your behavior, you can live in the identity of being loved. No matter what you've done, what you're currently doing, or what you will do, God loves you. He may not love what you do, but that doesn't mean that He doesn't love you. You are loved. Say it out loud. Say it a million times until it sounds like a foreign word. Do you know what I'm talking about? *Our minds are weird, man.*

You are loved.

And if someone makes you feel otherwise, please don't apply that to your identity. Just because people don't think you are worthy enough of love doesn't mean you aren't lovable. Maybe, just maybe, people can't love you because they don't even understand what love truly is anyways. Maybe it has nothing to do with you and everything to do with their lack of understanding of what it means to love someone.

God loves you. He loves you so much. While you may still think you are unworthy of love, just remember this: He doesn't love you because you're worthy; He loves you because He is. He will never love you any more than He does in this exact moment. Take that in today and every day for the rest of your life.

You are loved.

REFLECTION QUESTIONS

1. What experiences or relationships have made you feel unworthy of love?

2. How do we know that God loves us?

3. How can you remind yourself daily that God loves you?

4. When the enemy tries to use other people to make you feel unlovable, how can you respond?

CHAPTER 12
TIME TO UNTIE THE "NOTS"

I am the Bread of Life.

John 6:35 (KJV)

I am the Light of the World.

John 8:12 (KJV)

I am the Door.

John 10:9 (KJV)

I am the Good Shepherd.

John 10:11, 14 (KJV)

I am the Resurrection and the Life.

John 11:25 (KJV)

I am the Way and the Truth and the Life.

John 14:6 (KJV)

I am the Vine.

John 15:1, 5 (KJV)

Danielle Axelrod

If you've ever been on a job interview or tasked with introducing yourself to your new homeroom class, you are well aware of the inevitable prompt that causes all of the anxiety: "Tell us a little bit about yourself."

I often struggle with this task. How am I supposed to summarize my entire being within a five-minute window? What bits are important? What could be left out? Does anyone even care?

If you've ever had the pleasure of partaking in this bit of self-reflection, you are subconsciously aware of the fact that we all have the same strategy for forming our answer. We all describe ourselves by things that we *are*—not something that we're *not*.

Maybe your claims sounded like this: "I am a soccer player. I have two brothers. I am a writer. I live in a small town. I work at a small Italian restaurant on the weekends."

I'm sure they didn't sound like this: "I'm not a painter. I don't have a sister. I'm not a tuba player. I don't live in Brazil. I don't work in construction."

It sounds funny, doesn't it? Defining ourselves by our "*don'ts*" doesn't give anyone context to what our strengths are, and they certainly don't give us confidence in who we truly are.

My list of what I lack is a lot longer than my list of strengths. Like I mentioned earlier, we weren't created to be all things. Imagine how hard it would be to be good at everything? How would you know where to specifically devote your time to?

So, wouldn't you say it's a little silly to fixate on the things that God hasn't called you to? Wouldn't you lovingly smack me if you saw me continuously sulking over the fact that I can't sing a tune? It's been clear, all of my life, that musical talent is not in my DNA. So, why should I spend time focusing on that? Wouldn't that just take away from me being able to find and develop the strengths I *do* have knit inside of me?

This is what we do, though. We fixate on everything we are not and decide that we don't measure up, we're not enough, and we can't be used by God.

It's not a sin to ever declare something you're not. It's completely okay for me to preface any karaoke session with the declaration that I am *not* a singer. This only serves as a simultaneous courtesy and warning to my listeners. The real trouble comes when we decide our identity is branded by these "*nots.*"

If I walked around deciding that I wasn't worthy because I'm not a singer, we would have a problem. If the first words out of my mouth when someone asked me about myself were, "Well, I'll tell ya what I'm not, and that's a singer!" that would be absurd and kind of weird, to be honest.

Maybe someone told you that you weren't something, and you started to believe it, even if it's not true. Maybe someone told you that you're not good-looking, or you're not good enough, or you're not smart enough. You know, those kinds of "*nots*" that are opinions but become truths of our identity because we rehearse them over and over again in our minds.

Can I challenge you to do something today?

Untie those "*nots.*"

Just because the enemy whispered a lie into your mind doesn't mean you need to believe it. Just because someone decided that you were not up to their standard doesn't mean that you need to be defined by that. And just because the truth may be that you are not something that you were never created to be in the first place, you don't need to identify yourself by that either.

Untie the "*nots.*" They are binding you up and keeping you from seeing all that God has for you.

Now, I know what you might be thinking: Danielle, not all "*nots*" are bad. I get that. When you say "I'm not afraid," or "I'm not depressed," or "I'm not dumb," those are all good things. But, by themselves, they don't hold much power. Without a contradicting statement that claims what you are, instead, they leave you with little confidence when you claim them.

Like I said before, it would be really odd if I introduced myself and said, "Hi, I'm Danielle, and I'm not a painter." I bet your next question would be, "Okay, that's great, but what are you?"

It is much more powerful to claim what you are. And for the places that you have to claim a "not," you can do so, but always pair it with an "I Am."

For some of you, that capital A has you nodding your head and saying "ah" as the pieces start to come together.

Remember when I talked to you about God's strength coming through in our weakness? And how it's okay that we're not perfect and that we aren't good at all things because this is where God does some of His best work? Good, I'm glad you're paying attention.

There are going to be days when your "not" statements are seemingly screaming in your face. You know the ones.

- "I'm not pretty."
- "I'm not talented."
- "I'm not confident."
- "I'm not strong."
- "I'm not good enough."

We all feel it. And to be honest with you, these are continuous thoughts that I face at least once a day at some point. Okay, more like 5,000 times.

To some extent, we need to accept that these are derivatives of the lies of the enemy. This is where knowing the Word is important.

"I'm not pretty." False. God says you are fearfully and wonderfully made. You are made in His image, and everything He made, He looked at and said, "It is good." Do you think He messed up with you and said, "Oops, well, guess that will have to do"? I don't think so.

"I'm not talented." False. Please go read the last chapter.

I could go on and on. This is why you need to find the scriptures that you can speak back at these "not" statements. But there is some truth in some of them. This is where the "I Am" statements come in.

"I'm not strong." Okay, there's some truth here. You may be stronger than you think you are, but there are certain situations that we face and certain weak spots that we all have where our strength is depleted. We are not strong in every situation. That's the truth. But you know what's cool? God is. I'm not strong, but God is. And He lives within you.

"I'm not enough." No, by yourself, you're not. It's just a fact. We're human, and we have faults and mess-ups that leave us undeserving every single day. I'm not enough, but God is. And He lives within you.

Whatever you need, God has it. Wherever you lack, God makes up for it. Whatever you feel you are "not," God is. And if we never felt inadequate, we wouldn't have to rely on His power and mercy to bring us through for His glory. If we felt like we had everything it takes to succeed, we would all build up mental shrines out of pride.

I am not the best writer in the world. My dad thinks I am (shout out to Keith), but let's face it, most people probably would not read my writing and deem me among the greatest writers in the world. Although, if you've made it to this point, you might like my style, which makes you pretty rad. Thanks for that.

Here's the thing: God never asked us to be the best in our area. He never asked us to be perfect in our gift. And I'll tell you why I think He did this.

1. First and foremost, God wants us to rely on Him. If we were amazing at all things, we wouldn't need Him. I think you got that part by now.

2. But second, I don't think He wants us to identify ourselves by our gifts.

I am a writer, but that's not all I am. I am Danielle. I am a child of God.

If both of my arms were chopped off tomorrow and I couldn't write anymore, my identity wouldn't change. If this book completely fails and only my mom buys a copy, my identity wouldn't change. I am not bound by a label based on the talent that God gave me.

I think this is the issue with much of society. People find their worth in and identify themselves by what they do. Then, when that temporary identity crumbles, they have no idea who they actually are or why God created them.

Do you ever wonder what ex-pro athletes are doing? I wonder if Derek Jeter is okay, you know? I mean, on the surface, he seems to be doing just fine. The dude is set financially and has a gorgeous family. But I'm talking about the inside. Do you think he's truly happy without baseball? Do you think he's at a place where he knows who he is in Christ, and that will be enough for him? I sure hope so.

What about you? If you lost your job or had a season-ending injury, would you still be okay knowing that God has a different plan for your life that isn't dependent on that one skill you were relying on?

I know it's a tough thing to ponder, and I'm not saying that God is going to rip everything away from you, but it's freeing to know that you are more than what you do. In God's eyes, it doesn't matter if you're the CEO or the janitor. You have an equal value to Him. You are His child, and He loves you just as you are. You don't need to prove anything to Him.

I know it's hard to wrap our heads around because society has it all backward, but just remember this: your identity is in who God is; I Am. That's who God said He is: I Am.

A man who can empathize with our feeling of inadequacy is my main man, Moses. I love this dude, for real, just in case you couldn't tell.

When God called Moses, He gave him a mission to go rescue the Israelites from Pharaoh. Moses' response looks a lot like ours, most of the time:

> *"Who am I that I should go to Pharaoh and bring the Israelites out of Egypt?"*
>
> Exodus 3:11 (NIV)

Now, let's look at how God responded:

> *And God said, "I will be with you."*
>
> Exodus 3:12 (NIV)

God didn't hype Moses up and tell him that he was some great dude or that he was worthy of being called. He didn't praise him and told Moses all of the great qualities He noticed in him. Instead, God pointed Moses' focus to the comfort and strength that His presence offers. It didn't matter if Moses was unqualified, fearful, or unworthy to be called. God would be with him.

Let's keep going. So, Moses, in his doubt, continued to interrogate God, probably hoping God would realize that He called the wrong dude.

> Moses said to God, "Suppose I go to the Israelites and say to them, 'The God of your fathers has sent me to you,' and they ask me, 'What is his name?' Then what shall I tell them?"
>
> God said to Moses, "I Am who I Am. This is what you are to say to the Israelites: 'I Am has sent me to you.'"

Exodus 3:13–14 (NIV)

At first, I thought this was kind of a lame answer. If I was Moses, I probably would've just stared at that burning bush and asked, "What? You are…what?" But that's just it. God is everything you need. If you need strength, He is your strength. If you need comfort, He is your comfort. He is everything you need.

The Israelites were living in captivity. They were slaves in Egypt, and I'm sure there was lack, pain, fear, and overwhelming hopelessness inside each and every one of them. They may not have even known what they were looking for or what they needed to feel whole. But God had it all. I Am. He is the Great I Am because there is nothing that He doesn't have to sustain you.

Your true identity is in I Am. Not in lowercase, I am. You are a child of the Great I Am. And that means that you are called, chosen, and loved. It's not a matter of performance or labels that you have taken on or given yourself. It's a matter of His ability to work through the places that you feel make you unqualified and turn them into declarations of His glory.

So, of course, the enemy wants you to focus on anything but that. Of course, he wants you to stare your weaknesses in the face for so long that they become what you identify yourself by. But when you can learn to identify your weaknesses and focus on the strength that Christ will give you through those weaknesses—the whole game is changed.

I want you to notice how I said "through" and not despite. Because here's the thing: I think we look at our weaknesses and say, "Okay, I'm not strong here at all, so that must not be what God has called me to do." Now, it is true that some weaknesses are signals that we shouldn't necessarily pursue that path as a career, but that doesn't mean God can't use them for His glory. For example, I have a weakness in the area of rhythm. I'm pretty much equivalent to the totally lame dad at a kid's birthday party on the dance floor. It's pretty obvious that I won't be on *Dancing with the Stars* anytime, ever—unless they are doing a spoof episode. Plus, I don't really have a desire to dance, other than being confined to the private space of my room with some old-school Taylor Swift playing and a hairbrush in hand.

I am the girl who sort of dreads (forgive me, Lord) the first song of worship because it's usually an upbeat song that all of the cool kids are able to sway to with perfect swag. Meanwhile, I'm cringing, praying that my hand claps align with the beat and that I don't look like an absolute fool.

So, it's probably pretty obvious that it would be completely frustrating for me to pursue a career in dancing because it's not my natural strength. However—and I really need you to get this—that doesn't mean that God can't use this weakness for His glory if He wanted to.

I'll give you a great example. We have a dance team at the church I grew up in. My mom, who so ungraciously did not pass down her dancing skills to her daughter, is the head of the team. So, of course, I joined. We had a big Easter production that we used to do every year, and the dance team made a few appearances throughout. What was the genre of dance for these performances, you ask? Great question. The answer: ballet.

Now, if you know me, you are probably counting how much money you have in your wallet because you would pay the big bucks to see this awkward chick attempt a plié (PS: I had to Google how that was spelled. Originally, I typed *plee-ay*. So, this should give you some context).

If you don't know me, let me present it to you like this: imagine any NFL player attempting to dance on his tippy-toes and leap through the air graciously. Okay, that was dramatic, but my body was built to shove girls over on the soccer field, not to look dainty in a tutu. But nonetheless, here I was, ready to minister through twirls and leaps, with glitter eyeshadow and white ballet slippers.

After the performance, my pastor, who's a pretty tough dude—like hunts-deer-for-fun tough—came up to my mom and told her that he cried (sorry for letting this one out of the bag, PR), watching her and I dance because he was so touched by it. My friends who came to see the show had a similar reaction. I expected jokes about my lack of coordination, but instead, I received a complete contrast of a response. They were moved by what God did on that stage. For me, it was the first miracle I had seen God perform in my life.

That was a dramatic joke, but still. Somehow, God used me in ballet slippers to minister to so many people. That was such an eye-opening day for me. I realized that God's glory could not be confined to human ability. I told you, I can't dance. But somehow, in some way, God poured out His love through my obedience to dance for His purpose anyway.

God might not want you to use *all* of your effort in an area of weakness, but that doesn't mean He can't use that weakness at all.

Now, I'm sure some people in the crowd did not find my dancing to be amazing. I'm sure if a scout from the best dance school in the world came to see the performance, they would scoff at my sad attempt at a plié. But if I was fixated on those few that were so focused on judging my ability that they completely missed the presence of God, I would be doing just the same thing: focusing on something worthless and missing God's presence. I may not be a professional dancer, but I am a vessel for God's glory. You may not feel strong in some areas, and your identity is not in your weaknesses, but that doesn't mean that God can't use them.

It's time to untie the "*nots*" and rework your "*ams*." You are a child of God, and no achievement or failure can change that status. How freeing is that?

REFLECTION QUESTIONS

1. What labels have you given yourself that you need to let go of?

2. Why is it freeing to know that your weaknesses don't disqualify you?

3. Why is it freeing to know that you don't need to prove yourself to earn God's approval?

4. How will you define yourself now, and how can you remind yourself to claim that identity in Christ?

CHAPTER 13

WHAT HAPPENS WHEN THEY STILL DON'T CHOOSE ME?

If you belonged to the world, it would love you as its own. As it is, you do not belong to the world, but I have chosen you out of the world.

John 15:19 (NIV)

Okay, so you've made it this far, and you've probably started declaring new truths over yourself and speaking more positively. Huge start, I'm proud of you! And even if you haven't, I'm still proud of you. But what are you waiting for?

Here's where the tough truth comes in. Just because you've read a few chapters on how to reclaim your identity in Christ and have applied a few changes in your self-talk routine doesn't mean you are exempt from facing rejection or attacks on your identity again. This isn't a workout-once-and-you're-suddenly-buff type of deal. There's a reason those don't exist. Real results take time, and lasting results require repetition. It's going to take work, commitment, and determination to set new patterns and fight against insecurity, but don't let that intimidate you. Tie up your sneakers and take things one day at a time. Remember, God has so much in store for you. Don't give the enemy the satisfaction of giving up before you get to see it all.

One of the best places for us to be, according to the enemy, is in a place of low self-worth and extreme self-pity. He knows that if we are so hyper-focused on how much we don't measure up, our focus is off of other people and all of the amazing attributes of God. This is the perfect place for us to abandon what God has called us to do: love Him and love people.

So, don't take it as a surprise if you continue to face trials that attempt to sabotage the progress you've made. I don't say this to scare you because you already know that with God, you have all of the tools to defeat the enemy's ploys. But I don't want to sugar-coat it because I can confidently admit that I was shocked to face more battles once I thought I "defeated" insecurity.

My my, what a naïve approach that was! The truth is, I don't think we'll ever feel completely secure. Since we will never measure up to perfection, we will always have something that we lack in, and insecurity is just too powerful of a tool to the enemy. But I do think we can properly armor up to defend its attack and recognize that just because we feel insecure doesn't mean we have to let that confine us or hold us back. The more we practice this, the quicker we will shoot down any lies that come crawling into our heads.

When I was younger, my brothers rarely called me by my first name. Instead, the word I should have written on every name tag on the first day of school, summer camp, or job should have been "sensitive." I don't think a day went by that I didn't hear one of them utter a "You're so sensitive!" my way. In their defense, I was. Did they need to worsen my insecurity by shoving that label in my face? Probably not, but that's a sermon for another time.

Set Apart, Not Aside

Let's stick to the facts. I did take everything personally (and if we're being really honest, I still do). I thought I just couldn't help it.

If you know me, this won't come as a surprise to you. I feel my emotions at a much larger magnitude than most people. I became well aware of that at the age of seven when I cried over having to kill a spider (even though I hate them) because his family would be waiting for him, and he would never come home. Pathetic. But it's the type of empathy that my heart is unapologetically drawn to. I love with a big heart because my heart beats on a big level. It's just how I was wired. So, in that case, my brothers got it right. I am sensitive. And while that can be an incredible gift, it can also be one of my biggest downfalls.

When I allow my sensitivity to turn into offense, I am opening the door for the devil to confine my identity to a label that someone else has written for me. If I let words that people spew at me erode my confidence, I doubt the truths that God has spoken over me.

Recently, I had just started a new job, and I was facing some insecurity, big time. I didn't feel confident in my new role, and the exhausting attempt of proving my worth to a whole new group of strangers was preventing me from standing in the confidence of who God made me to be. Apparently, this was rather obvious to one of our other team members. After a meeting in which she witnessed me completely shut down, she boldly suggested that I needed a lot more confidence than I had recently exuded. While she was right, I could feel the words beginning to seep past the surface of my flesh, morphing into lies and stinging the insides of my soul. That simple sentence turned into internal shouts that sounded a lot like: "You're not good enough," "You have no reason to be here," "You'll never be a leader," "Maybe you heard God wrong. This is not where you're supposed to be."

It sounds dramatic, but this is the domino effect that takes place when we allow words to turn into labels and identities that don't align with the Word of God. Just because I allowed insecurity to shut me down at that moment doesn't mean that God hasn't chosen me. Just because I didn't feel confident at that moment doesn't mean that God can't place me in a role of leadership. Just because it didn't feel good to hear those words didn't mean that I had to let those feelings hold me back.

If you'll notice, I didn't shoot down the new team member's observation that I could use some help on my confidence. I didn't neglect this area of my persona that could use some help, but I *did* decide that I wouldn't let it define me. There's a difference here. I might need to walk in a lot more confidence to grow, but that doesn't mean I'm useless.

You are going to fall short in some areas. And you are going to face opposition from other people all of your life. It's just a fact. They may even reject the parts of you that are in alignment with biblical standards. Unfortunately, this is the enemy's favorite weapon because your greatest weapon against him is knowing who you are in Christ. When you are confident not in your own ability but in what Jesus can do through you because of who He is, you are unstoppable. No weapon formed against you can prosper.

There will always be opposition. There will always be someone who judges, ridicules, and rejects you. There will always be critique and places where you fall short. Unfortunately, we can't control that. It's part of this fallen world. Thanks a lot, Eve—just kidding. Let's be real; we all would've eaten the fruit.

The point is, if you are expecting to ever come to a point in your life where absolutely everyone loves you and thinks you are amazing, you are going to be highly disappointed. That point is never going to come. Remember, even Jesus, in His perfection, was criticized, accused, mocked, and rejected. What makes you think you, with your lack of perfection, won't be? If that sounded harsh, I'm sorry. Really, I'm typing to myself here. But think about that for a second. If you're facing rejection or ridicule, you're in good company.

One area of my life that I struggle most with this is with the opposite sex. If a girl doesn't want to be my friend, I get upset, but I'll get over that quicker than I can when a guy doesn't like me. I will fixate for days on what puzzle pieces that make up my being are not lining up with his picture and spend countless hours trying to figure out what I can change to make me more acceptable to him. Let me rephrase that. I don't spend those hours: I waste them.

Call me pathetic if you want, but I know that, underneath it all, you do the same exact thing. We can't handle rejection because it insinuates that there is something that is not right with us. There is something that is chipped, broken, or dull with who we appear to be because that person put us back on the shelf. Or they took one glance and kept walking without even considering us as an option.

It's hard not to take that personally, especially when you develop feelings for someone else. It's even harder when they decide they like you for a little while and then decide you're not what they were looking for after all. Because there you are, left to pick up the pieces and wondering what you could have done differently or what you need to change to make them stay. It's hard because feelings are fickle, shallow, and deceiving. But even when you understand that and even when you think you have grown in that area, there is nothing like the sting of rejection. It hurts because it's personal. They are not just rejecting a part of you; they are willing to give up every piece of you because of the parts they don't deem "enough." That is enough to make you question your entire worth.

So, of course, it's going to hurt. Of course, you're going to have that sinking feeling in your gut and nausea that won't allow you to focus on anything else. Don't beat yourself up for feeling disappointed by rejection. I'm not saying that facing it will ever get easier. But there is freedom to be found and a quicker recovery span that takes place when you acknowledge the pain but simultaneously make a choice to break the bondage it's trying to take on your identity.

Our world today is so obsessed with shoving the notion that you have to "make a name for yourself" or devote countless hours to try and finally "make it" in order to be successful. Which, if you think about it, do we really ever "make it"? What does that even mean anymore? Because as soon as you get a promotion in any area of life, you are on to yearning for the next thing. We tire ourselves out to gain more power, status, and wealth, and then we realize how unfulfilling it actually is, so we strive for even more of it. How smart are we?

As these messages get shoved down our throats, not just from social media but from a lot of the people in our lives, we start to believe the lie that we have to gain acceptance based on what culture's standards are, rather than standing on biblical truth. We start to lose our identity in Christ to try and increase our likes on social media and gain popularity with people. We try to impress the people around us by fitting in with the world's views and end up wondering why we feel so lost, sad, and unfulfilled.

When I started to develop my relationship with Jesus deeper than the occasional Sunday morning visits, I began to notice a drift in my friendships. I felt more fulfilled but less accepted by the people around me. My Instagram post likes took a dive when they were captioned with Scripture rather than the latest pop song lyrics. Did it feel good? Of course not. I'm human. But I had a choice to make. Was I going to stop displaying my faith in Jesus for fear of rejection from people who don't even know who He is? Or would I continue to share the Gospel and be okay with God removing the temporary affirmation?

To say that I never think about people's opinions of me or how much attention I get from social media would be a lie. Of course, I still think about these things, and of course, I still struggle with the feeling of unworthiness. But the more I intentionally remember Jesus and how lonely and rejected He must have felt most of the time, the more I realign my focus to fixate on the privilege it is to be able to share the good news with a broken world. I would rather lose a few friends and followers than lose out on the glorious works that God can do through my life.

If you feel like an outcast or like you have a different viewpoint than everyone around you, don't automatically shoot that down as a bad thing. You are in good company. Jesus had twelve followers. Twelve. That's it; twelve people who were wholly devoted to Him and saw the calling God had placed on His life. And yet, they still failed to see Jesus for all that He was. There were times when they didn't understand what Jesus was doing. There were times when they didn't agree with Jesus' actions or thought He was downright crazy for breaking cultural codes. They loved Jesus, but they never dictated Jesus' actions, and their praise never fulfilled His calling.

Jesus knew His assignment. He knew His purpose, and He knew the voice of His Father. He didn't need the affirmation of people, and He didn't need permission from anyone but God to fulfill the purpose He came for.

Do you think it hurt Jesus when the same people who praised Him in the streets with "*Hosanna!*" changed their chants later on to "*Crucify Him!*"? While Jesus was fully God, He was also fully man, which should come as a relief to us because the Bible tells us that He:

> *Had to be made like them, fully human in every way, in order that he might become a merciful and faithful high priest in service to God, and that he might make atonement for the sins of the people. Because he himself suffered when he was tempted, he is able to help those who are tempted.*
>
> Hebrews 2:17–18 (NIV)

We can find solace in this because Jesus understands our suffering. He understands the pain of rejection. He understands the temptation to lash out in anger and defend yourself from those who mistake your identity. He understands the heartbreak of having those closest to us misunderstand or turn their backs on us.

You don't have to pretend like rejection doesn't hurt. You don't have to pretend it's easy to feel loved when nobody seems to love you back. You can be honest and bring those feelings to Jesus because He understands.

It's so important to know what to do with those feelings when they come because there is no cure to prevent them from entering your life. If you let them linger, they will tempt you to settle for living a life less than what God has intended for you. However, when you know where to place them when they come, you are not allowing them to hinder you from walking in confidence and taking hold of all that God wants to bless you with.

I won't lie to you; I struggled with this just the other day. A few coworkers and I went to lunch, and as everyone told their majestic, Hallmark-scripted, successful love stories, I felt the familiar feeling of unworthiness barge through the door of my heart. Clearly, there was something wrong with me. All of these beautiful ladies found seemingly perfect knights in shining armor because they deserved them, and they were pretty, smart, funny, and skinny enough to be worthy of that kind of love story.

Then came these thoughts: Maybe I should just settle for the first guy that pays attention to me. Maybe I should be more docile. Maybe I should be less "dude-y." Can we add that to the dictionary, please?

See how this works?

I let a feeling of envy and unworthiness spiral into a place that suggested that I settle for something less than what God intends for my life.

I can't tell you when I'll get my successful (keyword here) chance at this whole love thing, but I can tell you that I've prayed with too much faith and assurance that God has the exact timing figured out and that whether or not that guy is in my life right now, I can't base my worth off of his love for me. I need to learn how to feel loved, just as I am right now. I need to come to terms with my bold personality, lack of rhythm, and pointed nose.

I need to walk in the confidence of who God made me to be without settling for something or someone that can never determine my worth.

If you're struggling with that today, you're not alone. But just know this: another person may love you, but their love is conditional and will undoubtedly fail you at some point. When you know that God's love for you isn't based on anything that you can do, you won't rely on human love to sustain you.

You cannot leave your worth in anyone else's hands. And guess who else is included in "anyone else"? You. No one else gets to define if you're loved, chosen, or acceptable, and you can't hold the weight of that either. But that deserves its own chapter. We'll get into that next…

REFLECTION QUESTIONS

1. What are you relying on to determine your worth? Have you let people hold that responsibility? How can you release that today?

2. Why is it comforting to know that Jesus understands suffering? What feelings are you struggling with today that you can bring to Him to help you with?

3. Why does the enemy want you to feel worthless?

4. Next time you feel lonely, what can you do to combat that feeling?

5. Find a passage in one of the Gospels (Matthew, Mark, Luke, John) that illustrates a time when Jesus was rejected, misunderstood, or ridiculed. Take notice of how Jesus responds. How does this relate to our own times of facing these same hurts?

CHAPTER 14

THE I IN INSECURE

So I find this law at work: Although I want to do good, evil is right there with me. For in my inner being I delight in God's law; but I see another law at work in me, waging war against the law of my mind and making me a prisoner of the law of sin at work within me. What a wretched man I am! Who will rescue me from this body that is subject to death? Thanks be to God, who delivers me through Jesus Christ our Lord!

Romans 7:21–25 (NIV)

The first thing I did after I read a book years ago about insecurity and rejection was decide to take things into my own hands. I was determined to find my worth. I was motivated to change my thinking and show the world what I was really made of. I was empowered to squash the little insecure bug I was, and everyone would notice how confident I was. I wouldn't care a thing what people would think, and no rejection would hurt me. No one would stop me!

It seems comical to type out, but it was the reality of my thoughts, and unfortunately, most people deal with the same outlook. As I mentioned in an earlier chapter, I cannot stand "self-help" books because the notion that we can change or grow solely by our own strength is a false concept that leaves so many of us feeling discouraged, disappointed, and even more like a failure than before.

While it's true that we play an instrumental part in our own progression, it's also imperative to realize that you are not going to transform overnight or all by yourself. There's a reason that Philippians 4:13 (NKJV) doesn't end after "I can do all things." The emphasis here is "through Christ who strengthens me."

Sure, your decisions, motivation, and dedication to the process are up to you, but if you are not bringing the grace, wisdom, and power of Jesus into it, you won't see any sort of lasting change.

When you acknowledge that you need Jesus, you are opening a door for grace to fill the gaps where you feel weakest and building a barrier to the pride that is seeking to take selfish credit for your progress.

See, we get it backward. We think that we need to do it all in our own strength and then show God our finished product. We think that we need to get it all together before we can boldly present ourselves to God and ask Him to use us for His glory.

To be honest, I almost didn't finish writing this book. About halfway through, when I started dealing with extreme insecurity in my personal life, I felt like the biggest hypocrite in the world. How could I be publishing a book on how to walk in confidence and not let others' opinions bring you down if I was clearly far from an expert in the topic? God, I think you got the wrong girl.

But God showed me something pretty powerful. I was trying to change myself without His help. I was trying so hard to become a confident woman and publish this book so that I could impress Him and show Him I was worthy enough to help others in this area. Once I felt the sting of rejection completely overtake me again, I shrunk back. Maybe I wasn't ready to help others.

Maybe people wouldn't find me credible because of how much I still struggle with feelings of inadequacy.

Remember Paul and his thorn? There are some things that we will struggle with more than we'd like to, but God reminds us that His grace is sufficient for us. God may not completely remove a struggle from our lives, but His presence will always be enough to help us through it. I'm not saying this as an excuse to stay in a state of insecurity but, rather, as a comfort for the times when we do find ourselves struggling, even amidst a time of immense growth.

In Romans 7, Paul talks about the conflict between our flesh and spirit. Even though we want to do the right thing, our flesh will fight us out of its natural sinful state. This is where we need to rely on God. While it can be disheartening to fail or struggle with the same thing over and over again, it's relieving to know that God is not mad or disappointed in us when we do struggle. He designed us to be dependent on Him. You weren't created to do this on your own. Again, this doesn't excuse us from staying in that struggle, but it breaks the shame that is trying to suffocate your worth.

So, if you find yourself frustrated because you've read the majority of this book and still seem to struggle with confidence, receive grace. Ask God to help you see the places that you need Him to take over, and keep working on the pieces that He has asked you to cover.

Keep reading the Word, keep declaring scriptural truth over yourself, keep praying for God to strengthen you. Stop beating yourself up for letting negative thoughts and feelings keep you down every so often, stop hiding in shame from God when you do mess it up, and stop trying to do this on your own and impress God.

You are growing more than you think you are.

When you take the "I" mentality to change (*I* have to, *I* should have, *I* need to…), you will end up walking in even more insecurity because your shortcomings and failures are completely in tandem with your own effort. But when you recognize that apart from God, you can't experience true inner change, you are able to release the burden of self-reliance and witness freedom in so many areas of your life.

I remember being asked to guest speak for an online service for a local church. Now, I had gone to school to be on-camera personnel, so my response should have been an easy, breezy, "Yes!" However, my "yes" was a bit hesitant and shaky because I was well aware of the inevitable stage fright I always experience—the kind that makes my legs wobble and my heart race before every on-camera appearance. As the days grew closer to my preaching debut, I contemplated calling the pastor and backing out. I had no idea what I was doing. I didn't even remotely know how to put a "sermon" together.

Plus, I didn't want to make a complete fool out of myself on camera, which was bound to happen when nerves were involved.

But something deep down inside of me knew that I couldn't walk away. I had to face my fears and rely on the Holy Spirit to deliver the Word that He had nestled inside of my heart for months before my opportunity to speak it alive came.

Sure, I still felt like I was going to throw up when they introduced me for my segment, but I stepped out in faith, which helped the words I spoke somehow come together to release the exact message God had put on my heart.

I had a part to play, which was using my strength of biblical study and preparation, as well as opening the big mouth the Lord gave me when it was time to, but I let go of my need to rely on my own strength to fight my nerves, and somehow, sounded like a girl who had preached a few times before.

I gave God what I had, and He filled in the rest. He allowed my mouth to be a vessel for His glory.

If I had done it all in my own strength or found confidence in my own ability to put together a message and charm the crowd on camera, my own efforts would have been praised, and there would have been no anointing on the words I spoke.

I rather rely on God to anoint my words and leave a lasting impact on someone's soul than impress a few people through my own empty ability.

This book is another example of that.

There was always a mental battle happening whenever I would set my mind to sit down and write it. A voice of doubt would convince me that I needed to impress the world with my craft. I began to listen to that voice over the still, small *voice* that promised to fill these pages with words of impact. My obedience to use my skill would offer something that was much more valuable if I focused more on doing it with God for people than as something to impress God and people.

This book isn't supposed to be about me and my craft. It's supposed to be about glorifying God and the love, joy, and freedom He offers when you recognize your worth as His child. As I let go of my need to impress y'all with fancy metaphors and big words that make me seem more credible, I allow a space for the Holy Spirit to pour out the words that He wants to impress on your heart.

You don't need to impress anybody with your skill. You need to let God use your skill to impress what He has for them on their hearts.

The other "I" mentality barrier that is blocking you from walking in full confidence in who God has created you to be is your lack of human ability to fully see yourself as God sees you.

When God looks at you, He is looking at you with absolute adoration. He sees all of the plans that He created for you and the extensive potential He knit your being with. He knows every little detail about you and sees all of the places, people, and opportunities that He has and will intentionally place in your life to live out the purpose He has specifically for you.

God also knows every mess-up you will make and every weakness you have that keeps you reliant on His strength. He didn't make an error when He chose you to be in the exact position you are in right now. He didn't make a mistake when He thought up every detail of your life and everything He would entrust you with. He knew you wouldn't carry it all perfectly, and He knew that not everyone would approve of His choice. But He chose you anyway. He sees more in you than you could ever see in yourself. And that's the truth you need to derive your confidence from, not your own feelings or personal standards.

It's hard to accept because it doesn't make sense. It's a confidence that is only manifested by faith. And true faith is believing what you can't always see.

Did you know that the thoughts God has about you are more than the grains of sand? Have y'all seen a grain of sand? It's tiny. I mean tiny, tiny. And if my math is correct, there's like a bajillion million times infinity of them on this earth. That's how many thoughts God has concerning you. I don't even think about ice cream that much, and ice cream is the love of my life.

Ephesians 1:11–12 (NIV) reminds us that "In him we were also chosen, having been predestined according to the plan of him who works everything in conformity with the purpose of his will, in order that we, who were the first to put our hope in Christ, might be for the praise of his glory."

That word, "predestined," always stops me in my tracks whenever I read these scriptures. Isn't it crazy to think that God had a purpose picked out for your life before He breathed life into your body? He chose your life to be an illustration of how merciful, loving, and redemptive Jesus is, and He chose the unique path you would walk in order to display that. You are chosen. You are loved. And there is absolutely nothing you can do to earn that.

If you're struggling to wrap your mind around that and truly believe that, you're not alone. It's hard to receive love when you feel so unlovable. It's hard to believe that someone could love every piece of you, especially when others have always made you feel small and worthless.

But it's the truth. Jesus loves me and you, this I know. The Bible tells me so.

So, in those moments where you feel like you aren't measuring up or like you are unworthy to be anyone's first choice, know this: God chose you. The Creator of the Universe thought every detail up about you and brought you into this world to serve a purpose that is far greater than you could ever imagine.

Honestly, I believe that we don't even know how much impact we are having on the people around us, and we won't know until we get to heaven. We aren't going to know every way that God used us in this life, but believe me, He is using you—all of you—every strength, broken piece, weak spot, and mess up to fulfill His purpose.

You weren't created to become a perfect specimen so that God can use you for greater things. You were created to do greater things, even in your imperfection, so that God would get the glory.

If the enemy can keep you focused on what people don't see *in* you, he can distract you from the glory that God wants to gain *through* you.

So, if you ever feel like you're not enough—it's okay. You don't have to be because God already is.

Let go of the need to gain validation from the people around you, including yourself. You are already loved and chosen by God. And once you impress that on your heart, it will always be enough.

REFLECTION QUESTIONS

1. What are you trying to do in your own strength that God wants you to hand to Him?

2. How does knowing you were chosen by God before you were born set you free from having to earn His love?

3. How can you remind yourself that God loves you unconditionally this week?

4. In what ways do you feel that you're not enough? How can you release those to God?

5. Write a prayer to ask God to help you feel and experience His love in a new way. Continue to journal about the different ways He reveals Himself to you this week.

ABOUT THE AUTHOR

Danielle Axelrod is originally from Poughkeepsie, New York, where she would scribble stories on any piece of paper she could find since she was five years old. When she isn't writing, you can probably find her on an athletic field or reading in a local coffee shop. Her experience in television production, writing, and teaching led her to her current job in social media as a content manager. Danielle lives in Charlotte, North Carolina, with her dog, Molly Rue. This is her first published work.

Danielle Axelrod

Printed in the USA
CPSIA information can be obtained
at www.ICGtesting.com
LVHW021831230823
755929LV00016B/635

9 781685 562724